D.O.R.

A MEMOIR

Vince Daley

Published by BookLocker.com, Inc., Bradenton, Florida.

BookLocker.com, Inc.
2013

First Edition

D.O.R.

A Memoir

By: Vince Daley

Table of Contents

PROLOGUE

The Viet Nam War era has proven to be the defining event for those of my generation. It represented not so much a coming of age for all of us as much as it meant an end to idealism, hope, and whatever other illusions may accompany the ideological mind set. From a purely personal perspective, the war first registered its impact on me in the early to mid-sixties when I was a student at Fordham University and the effects continued until the mid-seventies. During that period of intensive U.S. involvement in Viet Nam, I attended college, graduated, worked for a year and a half, served two years in the Marine Corps, married, was discharged, went back to work as a civilian, and divorced. By the time that 1976 had rolled around, I had married again and started graduate school.

Those of us who had started our college years during John F. Kennedy's term of office could not help but feel that the world would become a better place. Kennedy appeared to be an enlightened and compassionate president. Unfortunately, none of that was to be.

Following Kennedy's assassination and Lyndon Johnson's ascendancy to the presidency, we still felt that there was hope as Johnson's administration spoke of the possibility of discontinuing the military draft, further developing the domestic economy, and ensuring the civil rights of all citizens. With the Gulf of Tonkin Resolution and the attacks on Bien

Hoa in 1964 and the subsequent landing of Marines in Viet Nam in 1965, however, our hope for a better world dissipated quickly. The U.S. seemed to enter a period of downward spiral from a moral, ethical, political, and economic standpoint, from which it would not recover for many years. As the United States, continued to spin, seemingly out of control, the lives of many of its citizens seemed to follow a similar path.

What follows is the story of the two frustrating, and, at times, humorous years, that I spent in the Marine Corps from January of 1968 thru January of 1970. To say that my plans did not develop as expected would be the classic understatement of the day. Fortunately for me, my two years were spent stateside, rather than in Viet Nam. Others were less fortunate. Many served in Viet Nam and emerged physically unscathed but emotionally scarred. Others served and were either wounded or killed. My own experience provided a somewhat unique perspective that tended to bridge the gap that had developed between what was happening in civilian life at the time with the impact of a brutal and futile war. I was in the military but not in combat so I could relate somewhat to the civilian point of view. At the same time, being an enlisted man in the military I could also sympathize with the plight of the poor "snuffy" who had been unlucky enough to, not only end up in the military, but also in combat. I was also fortunate enough to serve with intelligent, talented "draftees" who simply wanted to go home alive and in one piece as well as with a group of individuals that had chosen to say no to a commission in the Marine Corps. I was a member of the latter group, having "come to my senses" during a three-month stay in Casual Company at Quantico in early 1968. We were known as "D.O.R's" or those who had decided, for one reason or another, to 'drop on request" from the program. In some cases, the individual just "couldn't hack it", physically or mentally. Others, myself included, had been injured in training, spent several months in Casual Company, and simply wearied of being "jerked around" by the Marine Corps.

Perhaps, I was simply too naïve when I enlisted or perhaps my personal expectations were too high. And then again, maybe, it was all simply brought about by the urgencies of a very messy war. In many ways it truly was a very painful two years and I wouldn't have minded missing the experience. On the other hand, I might have gone through life castigating myself for not having served during the Viet Nam War. At the very least, it was certainly an unusual experience and provided me with the material upon which this book is based.

I believe that the experiences of that particular period of our history can best be summed up by the following words:

**As the years come and go
Names in stone row on row
Images alive in their gaiety
Ever young in our memory**

**The lesson now so clear to me
War's cruelties once set free
Select its victims absent care
Pain sufficient for all to share**

Excerpt from the poem "Viet Nam" by Vincent Philip Daley

CHAPTER ONE

NO GOOD DEED GOES UNPUNISHED

After forty-five years, I still think back on it now and again and wonder how it all came about. It still never ceases to amaze me that I actually spent two years as an enlisted man in the Marine Corps. Seeing me as I am now, I'm sure my children can't picture it either. To begin to understand, you really have to go back a lot of years to a time when our country had not yet lost a war and people were still wrapped up in the nostalgia of World War II, only slightly besmirched by a blip, an aberration, known as the Korean War. Those were days when we still believed everything that our government told us. John Wayne still stormed up Mount Suribachi in "The Sands of Iwo Jima", William Holden attacked "The Bridges of Toko Ri", and Van Johnson and Spencer Tracy bombed Tokyo from B-25 bombers launched off the deck of the aircraft carrier Hornet. It was certainly a happier, and, perhaps, more foolish time that had followed World War II and carried us gently through the fifties. Unfortunately, all of that was about to end and most of us never saw it coming.

With the exception of the fact that the war in Viet Nam had been escalating rapidly for more than a year, my graduation from Fordham University in 1966 still offered many promising prospects. I had been accepted for graduate study in Economics at Fordham and I had also been offered a job with Texaco as a computer programmer trainee. Given the situation in Viet Nam, there was no question that all of us in the graduating class of 1966 were "standing in a draft." In those days there were only a few safe places to be. The first was in school with a "2S" deferment. The second, believe it or not, was in the Reserves or the National Guard. The Pentagon, in its infinite wisdom, had decided to fill its military ranks with draftees and volunteers, rather than activating the Reserves. The final "safe house" was "married with children."

My personal game plan was relatively simple. I would accept the position with Texaco, work there for the summer in order to make some money and then return to graduate school in the fall, protected by a student deferment. It wasn't that I was unpatriotic but spending two years in the military seemed very inconvenient at the time, particularly for a war that didn't seem to draw much interest or concern from either our government or the civilian populace. According to the government, we were winning big and it would all be over soon. Most families watched the hostilities as part of the evening news and failed to get too excited about it unless they happened to see a familiar name on the casualty lists. Ultimately, that is what would end the war. The fact was that it began to get too close, to touch too many people that we knew and loved. But that's another story.

Unfortunately, along the way, I had become quite comfortable with the money and the life style while working at Texaco and, once the summer had ended, I did not return to graduate school. At the tender age of twenty-three, I really had not thought all this through too carefully and it didn't take long for the draft board to catch up with me. They were not amused. By the time that October had rolled around, they had concluded, quite correctly, that I was not attending graduate school and that appeared to piss them off a bit. In those days, pissing off Selective Service was akin to pissing off the IRS. Within twenty-four hours of a phone call from Selective Service to my parents' home, at which time my father refused to divulge any information about my activities and my whereabouts, I was promptly reclassified from "2S" to "1A". For those not familiar with the doings of the local draft boards in those days, "1A" was the "kiss of death." That meant you had essentially been classified as "potential cannon fodder." They also were kind enough to schedule me for a pre-induction physical in early December at Fort Hamilton in Brooklyn, New York.

As I arrived at my local draft board office in Freeport, Long Island, in early December for transport by bus to Fort Hamilton, it looked like "old home week." I ran into many old friends from high school, all of whom seemed to have a note in hand relative to being excused from military service due to some medical condition, marital status, or educational studies. To be honest, I felt quite naked without a note of some sort explaining why I was not fit to be drafted. I need not have been concerned. Upon our arrival at Fort Hamilton, all notes were summarily dismissed as nonsense by either army doctors, officers standing by, or smiling NCO'S. Many potential draftees were virtually brought to tears as they saw their notes torn to shreds and trashed before their eyes, "What's this? You have a bad back? No, you're all right.", "Sorry, sonny, nine college credits ain't enough. You need twelve.", "Being married don't mean nothing unless your sugar is pregnant."

More than one candidate went home with a new resolve to get his wife pregnant. When the physical exam was completed, one of the NCO's gleefully shook my hand and said, "Congratulations. You passed with flying colors. You'll be in by Christmas."

My response was brief, "Thanks a lot."

Curiously, when I advised my employer, Texaco, of my dilemma, they suggested a surprise alternative. The government, always difficult to understand or predict, had decided to grant draft deferments to computer programmers because of an apparent shortage of programmers in the work force. Texaco asked for my permission to submit my name for a possible deferment. I agreed resignedly, not really expecting anything good to happen. One of my co-workers at Texaco, Pete Rader, was also approached relative to submitting his name. Pete was married and had received a deferment at the time as the sole support for his mother. He didn't think that his existing deferment would hold up over the long term and so he "took a shot." I was single and the sole support of only myself. The draft board, acting wisely and fairly as always, granted me a deferment, classified Pete "1A" and immediately drafted him. I felt more than a little guilty attending Pete's going away party with my new "2A" classification tucked safely away in my wallet.

During the following year, my younger brother Paul, who had dropped out of college, enlisted in the Marine Corps, the war in Viet Nam heated up dramatically, and I became engaged to be married. By the time that the engagement broke up in late 1967, I had decided to enlist, either out of frustration over the broken engagement or a misguided sense of patriotism. To be honest, the former was probably more relevant to me than the latter at that point in time. During the course of the preceding year, I had taken the various written and physical exams for flight programs in the Navy, Air Force, and Marine Corps. Flying seemed more appealing than crawling through the mud. By the end of 1967, only the Marine Corps had approved the results of both my written and physical tests. The Air Force continued to call my home to schedule a flight physical at Stewart Air Force Base but my mother kept trashing their messages each time that they called. She was not a big fan of the military, particularly, when it involved one of her sons. The Navy had approved me as a Naval Flying Officer Candidate (Weapons Officer) but not as an Aviation Officer Candidate (Pilot). Making the assumption that all aviation programs were about the same, I decided to go with the Marine Corps. That naïve assumption is what would lead to my two tumultuous years in the Marine Corps.

I signed all six copies of my enlistment papers in New York City on December 11, 1967 with the assistance of a grizzled Gunnery Sergeant. When I completed my signing, he made a few notes to himself and said, "We'll have to notify your local draft board of your enlistment. You're draft classification is "1A", right?"

My response apparently took him back a bit, "No, Actually, I'm classified "2A". I have an occupational deferment."

Lowering his pencil, he looked up at me puzzled by something, "What the hell are you doing here? Why are you enlisting?"

I have to admit that the warning signs went up a bit at that moment but I chose to reply as sincerely as I could, "Well, there's a war on and I thought it was the right thing to do."

He continued to stare at me for a moment or two, perhaps looking for any other signs of mental illness before replying, "Sure! Got it! I understand."

It was then that I should have run. Unfortunately, I didn't. Shortly thereafter, I was sworn in by a major who closed by saying, "If I were you, I'd get in shape."

To be honest, up until that very moment, I thought that I was in shape. In the very near future, I would understand better what he had meant.

CHAPTER TWO

THE AWAKENING

What struck me first was how dark and cold it was. It was one of those winter mornings when the stars are still clearly visible in the sky. We had been rousted out of our racks at 4:45 AM and, now, forty-five minutes later, we were standing in a formation listening to a tall dark apparition dressed in green scream profanities in our faces. Reality has only now begun to sink in. At this very moment I am saying to myself, "What the hell happened? What am I doing here? I thought it was warm in Virginia. Jesus Christ, it's seventeen degrees out here."

We are now into the second week of February and I'm standing in a formation as a part of 2nd Platoon, "E" Company, 50th OC, MCB, Quantico, Virginia. This particular level of Hell is what is known as "The Annex." "The Annex" is a relatively remote location as compared to what is known as "Mainside" Quantico. I should also add that, in my considered opinion, Quantico itself is in the middle of nowhere to start with. I find myself in the unique position of having succeeded in saying "no" to both the Air Force and the Navy and "yes" to the Marine Corps. The thought rings clearly in my mind like a chapel bell, "I must have been out of my fucking mind!"

How long has it been since I was sitting in Schraft's on 43rd Street nursing a Jack Daniels on the rocks or waking up in the brownstone on 18th Street next to Sharon's warm body? I've only been here for two weeks, "God! It seems like two years."

It occurs to me that this is really only a bad dream and that if I close my eyes and shake my head, I'll wake up and all of this will be gone. Not daring to move my head while either Staff Sergeant Puida or Gunny Koppel are still screaming, I close my eyes for a moment and then open them again, "God! It's all still here. This is real."

I had arrived in the town of Quantico on the evening of January 28, 1968, after a leisurely drive down from New York in my '67 Sport Fury. Quantico sure didn't seem like much of a town compared to New York. Actually, it didn't seem like much of a town period. This is going to be home for the next ten weeks, or so I thought at the time. I checked into a small motel right next to the main gate for Quantico taking time to admire the replica of the Marine Corps Memorial, seemingly standing guard over the base. I knew that it was a smaller version of the original that stands in Arlington but it was still inspiring to see, all the same. I felt a little lost that first night, grabbed dinner in the dining room of the motel, hit the sack early, and fell asleep. The next morning I took my time getting going.

Check in time at Quantico was scheduled for 1:00 PM. I had a leisurely breakfast and drove thru the main gate at about 12:30 PM. I was dressed in a pinstriped suit, button down shirt, regimental striped tie, wing-tipped shoes and a raincoat. In my mind I was reporting to OCS, not Parris Island, and I thought that I ought to at least look like I knew what I was doing. That was my first mistake or perhaps my second. The first was enlisting in the Marine Corps. I checked into the personnel office, was looked up and down with some amusement by a black gunnery sergeant, and was then told to wait outside until further notice. Not exactly the auspicious welcome I had been expecting. That should have been the first hint that things were not going to be what they should have been. Over the next few hours, the "candidates" began to drift in. With the exception of the enlisted marines dressed in class "A" uniforms who had been accepted into OCS, I was clearly overdressed. Up until that point in time things had been fairly casual and informal.

After about three hours of people drifting in, things started to get formal in a hurry. Several NCO's appeared on the scene and the screaming started, not to abate for many weeks. They first called for a formation. The next order of business was to go into what appeared to be a small version of the PX to draw a bag of toilet supplies, grab your personal bags, and get back in formation. We were then told to ensure that all personal vehicles were locked and to stand by to board a bus that had arrived on the scene. There were clearly more people than could comfortably fit on the bus but that didn't cause a problem. They just herded everyone on, "Get your asses on that bus. Move it. Move it. You there dummy, get inside the bus. I don't want to hear no talking in there."

I thought to myself, "How about groans? Are groans permitted?"

I felt like a holocaust victim in a cattle car on his way to Auschwitz. This was unbelievable. It was also impossible to maintain any sense of direction as to where you were or where the bus was going. It was beginning to get dark outside and this further contributed to a loss of orientation. I had no clue as to where we were or where we were going. Finally, the bus stopped outside a series of squat red brick buildings and the shouting started again, "Outside. Line up. Move it. Move it, asshole. All zoomies over here!"

All but the enlisted marines looked puzzled. What the hell is a zoomie? "Listen up dummies. If you're MOS is 9900 then you are a zoomie. You are either an AOC or an NFO. That means that you think you are too good for us ground-pounders. Now get the fuck over here."

I then realized that all aviation candidates were being assigned to the first building, "Get inside dummies and line up at the foot of a rack. How you going to fly a plane if you can't follow simple instructions?"

About thirty candidates hustled into the first building and lined up at the foot of one of the double-decker bunks. It was then that we first met "The Red Baron". He was squat in build, had red hair and freckles, and wore the stripes of a gunnery sergeant with rows of ribbons on his chest. His name was Zimmer and he really did look "mad as a hatter." His face was red, his eyes bulged, his neck seemed too big for his shirt, and he seemed to have a sneer permanently etched on his face. I thought to myself, "This is definitely not a happy camper."

We were all lined up next to our bunks and he strode purposely up and down the aisle, periodically lunging at someone, to see if they would flinch. Most did. The enlisted marines looked relatively placid and he didn't seem to bother with them. Suddenly he stood in front of a kid from California who I would later learn was named Poulsen and screamed in his face, "What the fuck are you looking at? Are you in love with me? Are you some sort of wiseass?"

As he asked the last question, he grabbed Poulsen by the front of the shirt and slammed him back against the wall. To his credit Poulsen said nothing and looked pretty calm. Near as I could tell, Poulsen had done nothing but "The Red Baron" apparently felt that some sort of "object lesson" was in order. I thought to myself, "This is really nuts. Whatever happened to not laying hands on another enlisted man? This sure doesn't look like any OCS that I've ever heard about."

From here it continued to go downhill but in a more orderly fashion. An officer made his appearance at the head of the squad bay and "The Baron" stepped back quickly from Poulsen. The captain, who appeared to be Hispanic, looked quizzically at Zimmer but said nothing. There was also a general sigh of relief among the "candidates". If it was not audible, it certainly was discernible in the looks that crossed our faces. "The Baron" looking disappointed, quickly glanced down at the floor. I thought to myself, "Now things will get straightened out. Surely, this officer knows the score and will fix this mess."

Unfortunately, not a great deal was about to change simply because an officer was present. Captain Garcia stood at the head of the squad bay and spoke softly but directly, "We have to check your gear for contraband. No drugs or medications are permitted. Place your gear on your rack and open each bag."

I groaned to myself, "What the fuck is this? Are they kidding me or what? What drugs? What contraband?"

Something else was going on here. Contraband might be part of it but not all of it. The Captain, "The Baron" and one other NCO moved down the aisle checking everybody's gear. "The Baron" screamed at Poulsen, "You there, smart guy, get that shit can and bring it over here. That's it. Hold it up."

As they stopped at each bunk they went thru a whole litany, as they trashed any pills, after-shave lotion or whatever, "What's this? You don't need that shit? You ain't going to have time to take no medicine or put on any after-shave lotion. What's wrong? Do you want to smell good?"

I stood quietly as they approached, trying to look aloof and detached. Surprisingly, almost nothing was said to me. At first they couldn't find anything that appeared to be a problem. Finally, "The Baron" with a nasty smile reached over and grabbed a clothes brush with nail cutters and file inside the handle and dumped it in the can, saying, "You don't need that shit."

I thought to myself, "Fuck you, Baron."

At the same time, I was happy to see the group move on. The Captain, apparently noting that some of the items that were being dumped were of some value and clearly not contraband, added, "Don't worry. These items will be returned when you complete your training."

I almost laughed out loud as I thought, "Right. I noticed how you're taking time to put everybody's name on their stuff. What a bunch of shit."

"The Baron" gave me a funny look but he moved away. It was almost as if he could read my mind but he seemed to sense weaker prey down the line. One of his next victims was some kid from Wyoming who really did seem to be some kind of "momma's boy." His stuff included a robe, pajamas, slippers, medications, all sorts of toiletries and they were just killing him, "What the fuck is your story boy? Do you think you're on vacation here? Look at this shit. I'm going to be watching you boy."

Finally, they finished up this latest episode of jerking everyone around and they left almost as fast as they had arrived. The exiting shot from "The Baron" was, "Stow your gear and form up outside for chow. Do it."

We exited the squad bay in a hurry, joined the formation outside and were quickly marched to chow. Outside the mess hall we were forced to stand at attention, cut square corners, and close it up. As they like to say in the Marine Corps, "Asshole to bellybutton. Close it up. Move it."

The chow turned out to be pretty decent although we only had about ten minutes to eat it. We then returned to the squad bay, showered and hit the rack. The next two days things were pretty quiet and I thought, "Maybe the worst has passed."

After all, I thought, "This is supposed to be OCS."

But, I was wrong.

We were trucked up to "Mainside" several times over the next few days for all kinds of medical tests. We were all "zoomies" as they liked to say in the Marine Corps. That is to say flyers.

We repeated virtually every test that we had undergone before being accepted in the program and that was probably why we had reported early. We had just started to settle in one morning when, a tall red-haired staff sergeant who was ramrod straight and spoke with a hoarse smoker's voice appeared and hollered, "Bates, Carson, Daley, Peterson, Poulsen, and Smith. Grab your gear and fall in outside."

Such was our initial introduction to Staff Sergeant Anthony Puida, our platoon sergeant for the next ten weeks. Before long, Puida would soon make the "Red Baron" seem like an absolute pussycat.

CHAPTER THREE

THE FACE OF FORCE RECON

As we lined up with our gear in hand, Staff Sergeant Puida explained the deal succinctly, "You assholes are in 2nd Platoon, E Company. Grab you gear and haul ass down to the next squad bay. That's your new home."

As I studied Puida, I could see the ribbons and decorations on his chest. Among other things, he was wearing jump wings. Puida was Force Recon, the most elite group in the Marine Corps. They are both jump trained and scuba trained. They love "snooping and pooping" in the "boonies" and most definitely are considered special by themselves and by others. I have to admit that, at that moment, I was a bit concerned about having a platoon sergeant who was that "gung ho." Later on in "the program" I would come to regret it even more.

Shortly after we had hit the squad bay and each grabbed a rack, Puida wandered in a few times but, in general, he seemed pretty quiet and laid back. He walked in once and asked, "How many of you guys have a GCT that's higher than 130?"

For the uninitiated, "GCT" is the civilian equivalent of I.Q. Despite having a relatively high "GCT", I had learned very quickly that to stick your hand up for any reason or to volunteer for anything was a serious mistake. Accordingly, I said nothing. A couple of "eager beavers" stuck their hands up and Puida nailed them good, "Take those shit cans and wash them out."

Clearly, Puida was enjoying every minute of watching the expression on their faces change. Later that day, however, some other things changed and it wasn't for the better. There was a loud commotion outside and all of a sudden a stampede of bodies came flying down the middle of the squad bay. Those of us who were already there stood up tentatively but quickly came to attention as we heard Puida bellow, "Get inside now. Line up at the foot of your rack. You're at attention. Don't move. Don't talk. Keep those eyes to the front."

All of a sudden the squad bay was filled with about 50 bodies. These guys had to be the ground marines, I thought. Puida, a Sergeant E-5, and a Captain then proceeded to run us thru our paces, "Stand at attention. Keep those eyes in the boat. Do you understand?"

We answered weakly, "Yes sir."

Puida screamed, "Don't call me sir. Do I look like an officer? I can't hear you."

And so it went for the next hour or so. As Puida screamed, we bellowed in response, "Yes, Staff Sergeant."

Puida, the captain, and the E-5 walked up and down the squad bay lunging at each candidate to see who would flinch. They would get right up to you so you could smell their breath and lunge closer. If you flinched you were really "dead meat."

The next bit of entertainment involved jumping into the rack at the same moment and remaining at attention or in civilian terms motionless. That went on for about half an hour and it was particularly tough on the guys in the upper racks. They had to not only move quickly but leap up as well. Finally, they tired of that and after the last attempt Puida bellowed, "You will now sleep like that, at attention. You will not move. You will not get out of the rack."

He then flicked off the lights and left. Everyone stayed still for ten minutes or so until they were sure that he was gone and then guys starting moving around to get water and hit the head. I kind of lay there awake but really exhausted and soon fell off to sleep. But, I knew I had to be awake early tomorrow. I already had a pretty good idea as to what was coming.

I woke at 4:30 the next morning and lay in my rack in anticipation of what I expected to happen very shortly. At exactly 4:45, there was some movement in the front of the squad bay. Almost immediately the lights flashed on in the squad bay, GI cans were thrown down the middle of the squad bay, and the screaming started once again, "Get out of those racks. Move it. Move it."

Puida turned over a rack but fortunately the occupant was already out of it, "Get at attention. Now, I'm only going to say this once. You have four minutes to shave, shower and shit and don't nobody cut himself. Now, move it."

Fifty odd recruits scrambled for the head and the showers. Unfortunately only about ten guys could shower at once and there were no more than eight sinks. It was an absolute zoo. Guys were four deep at the sinks trying to shave and screaming, "Throw me some water."

I was in the same boat as everyone else and I did the best that I could but it was impossible.

Within a few minutes Puida was at the entrance to the head screaming, "Get outside. Stand at attention at the foot of your rack."

One kid had blood streaming down his face where he had cut himself shaving in at least three different spots. Puida spotted him and screamed, "I told you not to cut yourself, asshole."

The terrified candidate responded, "I'm sorry Staff Sergeant. I couldn't help it."

Puida kind of chuckled to himself as he screamed back, "Don't give me that shit. When I say don't cut yourself, that's what I mean. Do you understand?"

"Yes, Staff Sergeant."

Puida dismissed him in typical form, "Get your sorry ass out of here."

And so the first of many such days to come had begun and I was already asking, "What the hell have I done? Help me Lord."

But there was no answer from the Lord, only the sound of Puida screaming in the background.

CHAPTER FOUR

EVERY DAY'S A HOLIDAY

After those first few days of activities deliberately intended to intimidate the platoon, the daily training routine became fairly standard. Puida quit throwing shit cans down the middle of the squad bay and we now had more than four minutes to shave, shower, and shit in the mornings but there still was no wasted time.

The day always started with a run that usually lasted for about ten to fifteen minutes. Regardless of the weather, we wore starched utility trousers with bloused boots, a sweatshirt and a starched cover for the run. Following the run we did about ten minutes of calisthenics. Given that this was early February, we often were called upon to lay down in four inches of snow to do our sit-ups and pushups. During the balance of the day we would run the obstacle course at least twice and have at least one long distance hike or forced march that was a company-wide event. In between these activities we would march and do rifle drill. We never seemed to stop marching and doing rifle drill. Occasionally, we would attend classes on such enlightened topics as: "The Proper Way to Dig a Slit Trench." These sessions included little tidbits of information like, "Never dig your slit trench upstream from your camp." The

Marine Corps was always a source of new and valuable knowledge.

The long distance marches were themselves things of beauty, not easily forgotten. No one who has ever trained at Quantico will ever forget the infamous "Hill Trail." The hill is three and a half miles to the top, which, in and of itself, wasn't all that bad. On the other hand, the hill has a nearly forty-five degree incline and we double timed all the way. The Marine Corps had a rule of thumb that said you had to cover a specific number of miles in a specific number of minutes and arrive ready to fight. Since we were in training we were not going to be called upon to fight. Therefore, they wanted us to cover the requisite distance in half the time. You certainly couldn't argue with convoluted logic like that. We wore utilities, boots, field jacket, helmet plus liner, light marching pack, full cartridge belt and carried an M-14 rifle. The cartridge belt included two magazines, a bayonet, canteen and first aid kit. On those brutal runs up the hill trail, and runs they were, most of us were just about on all fours, grasping with our hands and pushing with our legs. The object, of course, was not to be a "straggler." If the platoon sergeant passed you up during the course of the hike, even though you might catch up and pass him, you were still a "straggler." The "straggler's chit" would become part of your training record for evaluation at the end of the fifth week. You also would be called out and berated by the platoon sergeant at the end of the day as a 'straggler" or one clearly making the platoon look bad. Our first time out, Puida passed me up briefly on the hill, but then I caught up and passed him. As I did so he sounded off loudly, "That don't mean shit, Daley. You're still a straggler. If I pass you up you're a straggler."

Whether this was truly the rule or Puida was just embarrassed that I had caught him again half way up the hill, was tough to tell.

Some of the other more interesting activities were climbing twenty-foot ropes situated at the end of the obstacle course in full gear. Given the fact that I was relatively light but still strong at about 155 pounds, I could handle the ropes pretty easily. Some of the bigger candidates, particularly those that were not in shape, struggled with the climb. I can remember one incident where the kid from Wyoming, call him Wilson, could not make it to the top of the ropes. The whole platoon had already completed the climb and we were standing in formation watching Wilson struggle to make it to the top while Puida berated him and drove him on, "Come on, Wilson. You fat piece of shit. Are you telling me that you can't climb that rope at least once?"

Wilson was now about eighteen feet from the ground, unable to climb further and struggling to hang on, "Wilson! You're not going to die on me are you?"

At that moment, Wilson lost his grip and tumbled backwards landing with a sickening thud on the back of his neck, cushioned only by his helmet and his pack. The platoon stared at Wilson, shocked by the fall and you could almost hear our thoughts expressed in unison, "Shit! That guy must be dead."

Puida, undoubtedly shocked and surprised as well by this sudden turn of events, did not move towards Wilson, who was now sprawled on the ground, but rather ordered quickly, "Platoon, Attenhut! About Face!"

We all now had our backs to Wilson. I knew in that moment that Puida had thought Wilson was either dead or seriously injured and, whether to shield the platoon from the sight or to limit the number of eyewitness accounts, had issued the order. Amazingly, Wilson was not seriously hurt. None of us could believe that he wasn't dead. Later in the program, Wilson and a few other candidates would be dropped from the platoon and assigned to a "PT" or Physical Training Platoon to get into shape. But on that particular day, he had been lucky. He was still alive despite a horrendous fall of fifteen to eighteen feet.

The winter weather was taking a toll on us, as well. It was wet and cold and we spent many hours outside and exposed to the elements. My fingers were so sore from the weather that I could barely button my shirt. Many members of the platoon became seriously ill. Some even contracted pneumonia. At one point, I was convinced that I had pneumonia as well. My lungs were so congested that I was having trouble breathing at night. I would continually flip from my back to my stomach, trying to sleep. Eventually, it appeared to dissipate in my case. But, it was not unusual to go to sleep at night and to have candidates carried out in the middle of the night. You would wake up in the morning to find the guy in the bunk next to you gone, usually to the hospital. If you were sent to the hospital, you were really sick.

One of my more trying training days was the Individual Movement Course, especially, what was referred to as "Quigley's Special." The Individual Movement Course was challenging by itself and the weather was, as usual, horrible. We had to jump up and run on slippery logs mounted about three feet off the ground. The logs were about thirty or forty feet in length. We also had to dive thru a metal chute mounted on a slope that dropped you about seven or eight feet at the end to the ground. Actually, you were supposed to go thru feet first but a few "huckleberries" were so fired up that they dived thru and Puida, amused by it all, insisted that we all dive thru. People came firing out of that chute at about thirty miles an hour and landing on the guys in front of them. We then had to crawl thru a sewer pipe that was about thirty inches in diameter and about thirty feet in length. There were guys in front of you and in back of you and it was slick inside the pipe. That one was a real horror for me, I'll readily admit. I kept trying to figure out how they would get us out if someone got stuck in the pipe with all the gear we had on. The guy in front of me weighed about two twenty and he looked like he barely could fit. That experience was one of the few that really did panic me. But, they saved the best for last in "Quigley's Special."

Quigley, himself was a first lieutenant. Actually, he was what they referred to as an "LDO" or Limited Duty Officer. Because the Viet Nam War was raging hard and fast, the Marine Corps was experiencing a shortage of officers, particularly for training purposes or stateside billets. Accordingly, they were commissioning senior enlisted men such as Quigley. Quigley actually had a permanent rank of Gunnery Sergeant. It warmed my heart greatly when I saw Quigley a year or so later at Camp Lejeune. He was walking around wearing sergeant's stripes. Quigley was obviously a "grunt" or what the Marine Corps referred to as infantry. He had put together the nightmare we were about to encounter based on his own personal experience and, perhaps, some imagination, as well.

"Quigley's Special" consisted of a conglomeration of strands of barb wire, concertina wire, and abatisus covering an area perhaps a hundred feet wide and a hundred feet deep. The object of the game was to traverse the field on your back pushing the wire up with your rifle, while under fire. The "fire" consisted of Quigley and others standing over candidates and unloading full clips of blanks right on top of them as they struggled with the wire and obstacles. Despite repeated orders to the contrary, panic quickly became the "order of the day." People began thrashing around in the wire. I caught a strand under my neck and couldn't move forward. As I backed off to clear myself and then started in again, Quigley, perhaps thinking that I was "retreating" stood over me unloading his M-14 right on top of me, "You better move. They're going to be coming in just that close."

Contrary to popular opinion, blanks fired directly on you do hurt. They sting and they burn. At this point I felt the rage rise up in me, partly because of the situation I found myself in, Quigley's actions, and probably, the implied insult thrown in my direction relative to backing off. By the time I emerged at the other side of the wire I was truly ready to kill. Our instructions had been to emerge from the field, charge up a hill and deliver a slashing stroke with our bayonets to a padded dummy planted there, followed by a vertical butt stroke. As I charged up the hill, I noticed Puida standing off to one side and laughing at our plight. It's funny but I can still feel that emotion today. My initial impulse was to charge Puida rather than the dummy and stick him. It was a close call, but, fortunately, I wasn't quite that far gone, yet.

And so our training went from one week to the next. With the exception of an occasional variation for a class or an exercise, it was always pretty much the same. We ran, we exercised, we marched and drilled with our rifles and we went on forced marches, or better yet forced runs. I can remember on one occasion double-timing with full gear for thirteen miles. When we stopped, all I could feel was the sensation of pins and needles in the soles of my feet. We became harder and we became stronger and in the process, we moved further away from being civilians and closer to becoming Marines

CHAPTER FIVE

LIBERTY FOLLOWED BY DISASTER

We were now coming to the end of our fifth week of training and we were sweating out what were known as "Fifth Week Boards." If for some reason a candidate's progress, either physically or mentally, was deemed to be unsatisfactory by his platoon sergeant and or his platoon commander, he could be sent up before a Fifth Week Review Board. That review could lead to a candidate being recycled into either a PT Program to get into shape or simply into another OC program. Given what we had all gone thru to date, no one wanted to be recycled for any reason. The end of the fifth week was also the halfway point in the program and, barring the unexpected, we had all been promised liberty. It would be a short liberty, from 2:00 PM Saturday until 6:00 PM Sunday, but liberty nonetheless, and we all planned to take advantage of it. The plan was simple enough. We would drive to D.C., check into the Sheraton, party Saturday night, recover on Sunday and return to Quantico on Sunday evening.

The upcoming weekend would also be an opportunity for me to reset myself physically and mentally and to consider my options. Puida had already cornered a number of us "zoomies" to ask if we would consider going to the Basic School, which was a six-month advanced program for ground officers, prior to going to flight school, just in case we were to wash out. I had advised that I wanted to go right to flight school. The other "scuttlebutt" going around was that only a very limited number of AOC's and NFO's would be sent to Pensacola to fly fixed-wing aircraft and that most of us would be sent to Army helicopter school. This last point really disturbed me since the expected life span for a helicopter pilot going into a "hot" landing zone or "LZ" was about thirty seconds. My contract with the Marine Corps called for me to train at Quantico for ten weeks and then go to Pensacola for eighteen months of fixed-wing flight training. After flight training, I would be obligated to serve three and a half years on active duty. There was no way that I was going to invest an extra six months in the Basic School nor would I go to Army helicopter school, if I had any choice in the matter. What really bothered me the most was the Marine Corps was changing the rules right in the middle of the game. All of this was on my mind as we moved closer to the halfway point in the program.

By now our platoon had been reduced to thirty men. We had lost in excess of twenty men through the attrition associated with illness, injury, or physical fitness. The other two platoons had only lost about ten men each and each of those platoons retained a contingent of about forty plus men. Puida seemed to take great pride in the high attrition rate for our platoon. The message was clear. He was "Recon" and, even though our platoon commander, Captain Miller was not, the company commander Major Duncan was also a member of that select club. I kept wondering if this assignment was Puida's first training command and he was just too "gung ho" or was he simply bucking for another stripe. In any event, our platoon had taken the lion's share of the manpower hits.

I also wasn't sure whether Puida planned to send me before the Fifth Week Board or not. He wasn't crazy about us "zoomies" to start with and I had already received at least one straggler's chit. Being a bit older at twenty-five and, hopefully, wiser, I wasn't quite as "fired up" as some members of the platoon but I did try to consistently give a good effort. Interestingly, I had the opportunity to stand "fire watch" one night with Puida in company headquarters and he had informally tried to draw me about the platoon, "So, Daley, what do you think of the platoon now?"

I hesitated and then answered as honestly as I could, "Well, Staff Sergeant, I think you have a lot of "hard chargers" in the platoon but a few strike me as "brown nosers" rather than really being "gung ho."

At this point, Puida went positively ballistic, "Bullshit! There ain't nobody in this platoon that's going to "brown nose" me. Not in my platoon! No one is going to get away with that shit. This platoon is going to be the best one in the company."

I decided at that point that honesty probably wasn't the "watchword of the day." But, perhaps, my comment had left him with his guard down somewhat, and, unexpectedly, he began to talk about Viet Nam, "Let me tell you something, Daley. All of you guys are going to Nam and ten percent of you ain't coming back. If you're not tough enough they're going to kill you over there. I have a friend who they shot nine times but they didn't kill him. Now he's going back to kill them. Another time, our platoon was on a search and destroy mission and we drew fire from this village. We went in there and killed every man, woman, and child in that village and burned it to the ground. That's what you have to do in Viet Nam."

I said nothing in response but it was clear to me at that moment that Puida and I were simply too different to ever be on the same page and I simply left it at that.

As it turned out, two guys were sent up before the Fifth Week Board. I was not one of them. Now there were only twenty-eight of us left in the platoon. That was just about half of what we started with.

By 2:00 PM on Saturday I had drawn a liberty card, and, with four other guys piled into my car, we were on our way to the Sheraton and D.C. We were all in civilian clothes but it was clear from the haircuts who we were. When I had drawn my liberty card, the buck sergeant on duty had questioned why I was wearing brown loafers with blue slacks but I decided not to argue with a man with such "obvious fashion credentials." Somehow, I found my way across the 14th Street Bridge into D.C. and located the Sheraton. The five of us must have been some sight checking in. We all had our hair cut high and tight almost bald and we were all carrying an overnight bag and field boots still to be shined before our return on Sunday. No one really showed any surprise upon our arrival and I'm sure they had seen it all before. Other hardened young men had been there before us, looking for a fling before returning to more arduous training and before finally being swallowed up by the war in Viet Nam.

A half dozen of us gathered in the hotel pub shortly after check-in for some hamburgers and a few beers. They were selling what was referred to as a "yard of beer" which was in essence a three foot tube full of beer. Some of the guys bought in but I wasn't quite up to it yet. I stuck to a beer or two looking forward to the evening downtown. One of the "zoomies" by the name of Barr chimed in, "There's a club located on "L" Street or "M" Street that's supposed to be knee-deep in broads. We can't miss there." No one objected and that became the agreed upon destination.

An hour or so later I went back to my room to crash for an hour or two before we got together in the lobby at 7:00 PM. That was my biggest mistake that weekend. When I next opened my eyes, it was morning. Saturday night had come and gone and I had slept through it in the most comfortable bed that I had been in since leaving home. The fatigue followed by a couple of beers had been too much for me. For the rest of the day over breakfast and lunch, I listened to all the wild stories of conquest that my compatriots had to tell about their night on the town. Whether they were lying or not or, for that matter could even remember what had happened, was tough to tell. Disappointed at having missed the night out but now well rested, I was foolish enough to think that this was the worst thing that would happen to me that week.

By late afternoon, we were back in the squad bay getting ready for our first "Admin Move." An "Admin Move" involves a forced march into the "boonies" carrying a field transport pack, pitching tents, performing some night exercises and returning the following morning. For the uninitiated, a field transport pack involves carrying everything on your back with the exception of your foot locker and wall locker. You have extra clothes, mess kit, blanket, tent half, soap, and shaving gear. The pack approaches sixty pounds in weight and you have to attach special suspenders to your cartridge belt to support it. For little guys like me, adding this pack to the normal gear of helmet, rifle, canteen, magazines, bayonet, and first aid kit, meant you were carrying about half your body weight.

I was convinced that, as loaded up as we were, they would not run us over the hill trail. Of course, I was wrong again. Up the hill we went and a number of us could not help but straggle. The weight was just too much. At the top of the hill, those of us who had straggled were listening to a "ration of shit" from a buck sergeant who was wearing a soft cover and a light marching pack stuffed with foam rubber, "You guys are stragglers. You bunch of pussies."

My mental response was succinct, "Up yours, asshole."

Still, I was surprised that I had straggled. I was certainly stronger than when we had started the program but I guess the weight of the pack was just too great or the program was simply wearing me down both mentally and physically.

We formed up at the top of the hill before starting our forced march further into the "boonies." Puida did not look happy with those of us who had fallen behind but he said nothing, which, in and of itself, was surprising. Then we pushed off and before too long Puida had our platoon double timing. I thought I remembered a regulation that prohibited double timing troops carrying a field transport pack but that didn't seem to bother Puida. And then, suddenly, it happened. I turned my left ankle and the weight of the pack brought my left ankle right down to the ground. The pain was excruciating and for a few moments I couldn't get up. I kept trying but I kept going in a circle, kind of like a pinwheel. People were leaping over me and on me as they tried to get by. Suddenly I heard the voice of the Company XO, Captain Mahoney. He really was a king-sized prick, well taken with himself, "You better get up you son of a bitch. We're just getting started. Get on your feet."

Somehow I managed to struggle to my feet and the pain in my ankle was extreme. I had twisted the ankle a few times in training but never this badly. As I ran, though, the ankle began to loosen up and some of the pain dissipated. The fact that I was wearing boots probably helped some. At the very least, it provided some support and I would learn later that it prevented swelling. When we reached our bivouac site, we paired off and set up our tents, each making use of our tent halves. They served hot chow in the field and as I walked around the ankle proved painful but bearable.

It was the middle of March and we were deep in the Virginia woods so darkness was not long in coming. Each squad then set out on a night compass march in almost absolute darkness with no lights permitted. If you turned on a flashlight for any reason the troop handlers were all over you. Direction was determined strictly by clicks on the compass, each one representing a fixed number of degrees and distance by a specified number of paces in the designated direction. As we were getting close to the end of the exercise it became clear to all of us that our squad was off course. We could see another squad nearby and it looked like we were going to cross their path at some point, if we kept going as we were. That had to be wrong. Less we miss the target, and trying to be a little slick, we decided to ignore our compass heading and began to meander in a general direction that would run us almost on a parallel course with the other squads. I was sure that we had messed up the clicks on the compass and I decided to think of this as showing some initiative. As a result of our finagling, we did pretty much hit the target right on.

Throughout the course of the march, the pain in my ankle had been worsening but I kept hoping that it wasn't broken. Carson, a member of our squad, suggested that I have it checked by a corpsman on our return to the bivouac area. Carson was an enlisted man of about twenty-six with the rank of staff sergeant who already had eight years in the Marine Corps. His MOS had been in data processing and he was now working on being a second lieutenant and a "grunt." I trusted Carson because he was pretty squared-away and the rumor had reached the platoon that he had tried to "D.O.R." but been talked out of it by Puida. My biggest fear, of course, was of being recycled because of injury. I'd already been through too much to get jerked around that way.

Unfortunately, Puida spotted me getting my ankle wrapped. I really couldn't see the condition of my ankle in the dark nor could the corpsman so he wrapped it and I barely managed to get the boot back on when I heard Puida bellow, "Daley! What the hell is the matter with you?"

I felt like a deer caught in the headlights as I responded, "Staff Sergeant, I turned my ankle while we were double-timing."

Puida didn't hesitate for a second, "You ride the truck back tomorrow, Daley. I don't want to hear nothing."

Clearly, his intent was to shame me but at that point I didn't really care. I doubted that even Puida could have taken the fall that I took, finished the march, and then walked on that ankle on a night compass march in the pain that I was in. I just stared at him and, perhaps sensing my anger, he almost said something but I simply replied, "Aye, Aye, staff sergeant."

I turned and limped back to my tent while Carson, having heard Puida looked at me but said nothing.

That night the temperatures dropped, it snowed, and my foot felt like it was frozen solid from the ankle down. It felt like a piece of ice at the end of my leg. I suspected that all the blood vessels were torn up and I wasn't getting much circulation. By morning I could only stand on one foot. You haven't really lived until you try to take a piss off the side of a hill while standing on one foot. Still, I helped to break down the tent and packed my gear. Carson could see that I was having a lot of trouble with the ankle and he and another squad member helped me down the hill to the truck. I climbed onboard and rode back to the squad bay. When we arrived and I hobbled off the truck, Mahoney spotted me and approached sneering, "What the hell is your problem?"

I didn't salute him and didn't say "sir." I just said, "I can't walk."

Mahoney looked stunned as he suddenly recognized me from the fall the day before. I hopped into the squad bay to wait for Puida and the remainder of the platoon, all the time wondering what was going to happen next. I finally managed to get my boot off and I removed the ace bandage wrapping. What I saw was not reassuring. My foot looked like a bell-shaped ham on the end of my leg. It was swollen and discolored. I could tell that I was in a lot of trouble. It would be a miracle if the ankle wasn't broken. My spirits fell even further. There was no way that I planned to repeat the last five weeks. I'd had it. Fuck the Marine Corps. There was no way that I was going to let them recycle me. There was no way that I was going to go to the Basic School and there was no way that I was going to go to Army Helicopter School. On the other hand, avoiding those options wasn't going to be easy. My spirits dropped even lower as I took stock of my situation. I was twenty-five years old. I had given up a good job and a draft deferment to enlist in the Marine Corps. I had put in five outrageously hard weeks of training and now my ankle was torn up. At that moment I was definitely not a happy camper.

In the midst of my reverie, I heard a huge commotion as the rest of the platoon came crashing into the squad bay. They tossed their gear and stood panting for a few moments. My bunkmates glanced in my direction and I could sense at that moment that I was now an outsider. I was hurt and could no longer perform as they could. They felt sorry for me but at the same time glad that it had been me and not them. They looked quickly away, clearly, feeling ashamed of those contrasting emotions, "How's the foot they asked?"

I shrugged and said, "Not great. I'm hoping it's not broken."

A few came closer to take a look, "Jesus Christ! I've never seen anything like that. You don't think that's broken? You mean you walked on that?"

Puida was now bellowing in the background, "That's it. You guys are it. I'll get rid of everyone else. Daley! Where's Daley? Get up here. I want to see that foot."

From his tone, it sounded like Puida had already decided to shit can me, "Here, staff sergeant."

Suddenly the squad bay was deadly quiet. Holding onto the end of the double-decker bunks, I hopped towards the front of the squad bay where Puida waited expectantly, "Let's see that foot. I want to see it."

As I stood in front of Puida and stuck out what had once been but no longer looked like a foot, I could see the anticipation on his face quickly turn to shock and something else. Perhaps, it was shame, "Jesus! What the hell did you do to that foot?"

My answer was succinct, "I twisted it while we were double-timing."

My words were short but my meaning was clear. For the first time since I had met him, Puida appeared at a loss for words as he stared at the deck, "Two of you guys take him over to sick bay right now."

The Navy corpsman, in response to my question as to whether he thought the ankle was broken, summed it up nicely, "Are you shitting me? I've never seen anything like that."

He promptly shipped me to the hospital for x-rays and, I was quickly fitted with a short leg cast.

Unbelievably, nothing was broken but every ligament and tendon had been stretched and numerous blood vessels had broken. It was pretty clear, even to me, that my days in the 50th OC were numbered, if not already over.

Within two days, Puida shipped me out to Casual Company. In an empty and now quiet squad bay, he helped me pack my gear and load it in my car so that I could drive up to "Mainside." The platoon was out in the field, involved in some training exercise. I had become an embarrassment to the platoon and the company. I was now a reminder of what could happen to any of them. The company commander and the platoon commander were both probably worried about how the report on the injury would read. For all of those reasons, I had to go. Puida even went so far as to help me pull a white sweat sock over the cast as he uttered a few reassuring words, "You've got a lot of good stuff in you, Daley. Don't give up on this."

When I walked out of the squad bay for the last time I was on crutches and I had tears in my eyes. They weren't tears of sorrow for an opportunity lost. They were tears of frustration and anger.

CHAPTER SIX

GREETINGS PILGRIM, YOUR SEARCH IS ENDED

When I arrived at Casual Company my mood was grim and I'm sure that my face reflected it. I felt like I had really been fucked royally by the Marine Corps. The first person that I encountered was a short stubby looking guy from Maine by the name of Hampton. He had been a member of our platoon but early on had either gotten sick or been injured in training. I couldn't remember which. One thing I did remember was that I had definitely categorized him as a "non hacker" or one that wasn't inclined to extend himself to any great degree. Noting the tense look on my face he still welcomed me, "Greetings, Pilgrim. Your search has ended. Relax man. You're out of the shit now. This is Casual, man. This is soft duty."

It was mid-afternoon and the squad bay was pretty empty. The Marine Corps in its infinite wisdom had decided to place its injured on the second deck of a building that was also the furthest from the mess hall. This I would learn very quickly. If you have ever had your leg in a cast, you know that a non-walking cast is the worst. You can't put any weight on the cast. Therefore, you have to use crutches to walk which, of course, ties up your hands. Climbing stairs to a second-deck squad bay or trekking the long walk to the mess hall on crutches is great for strengthening the arms but does not do much for your morale. Handling a mess tray, thus encumbered, is next to impossible. Fortunately for me, a few of my fellow members of Casual were willing to help out at the mess hall. Looking at the situation initially, I almost had the feeling that the Marine Corps was punishing us, the barely walking wounded, for having committed the grievous crime of getting injured. The fact that the training regimen might have contributed to the situation seemed not to have registered on the reigning powers at that time. Perhaps, they were merely sticking us in some remote location where we were not so likely to be seen. Whatever the reason, we were clearly outcasts. We had been ostracized, both physically and mentally. What is it that they say, "Out of sight, out of mind."

In truth, the accommodations were not really all that bad. It was still a sixty-man squad bay with both upper and lower racks or bunks, a foot locker, and two wall lockers for each person. The squad bays at "The Annex" had been single story buildings with concrete floors. These building were two stories high with polished wood floors on the second deck. Of course, we were the ones who had to keep the floors polished but you have to take the bad with the good. Behind the building a few hundred feet away flowed one of the tributaries of the Potomac River. Within a month or so of taking up residence there, I would see two Marine Corps F-7 Corsair fighter jets through the windows screaming up that stream of water, virtually at eye level, moving from right to left, before making a vertical climb. They were part of an air show being conducted nearby. For the moment, I must admit, I did feel a serious pang of regret for a lost opportunity. Over time, those feelings would become few and far between as I closed in on the end of my active duty.

As the afternoon passed, my fellow residents of Casual Company began to drift back in. Most were limping or wearing a cast on a foot or an arm. A few looked pretty healthy to me and I assumed that they were on the verge of being recycled into the next OC program. They were a strange looking bunch. At the far end of the squad bay and across the aisle were two guys from the west coast. One was a Hispanic named Robledo who was thumping around on a walking cast that looked like it had seen better days. Robledo was olive-skinned and had shaggy dark hair that hung over his forehead. His bunkmate was slightly built guy with light brown hair and glasses who looked like his right elbow was seriously screwed up. He wore no cast or bandage but the arm just looked a bit misshapen. I was told that he was a graduate of Stanford Law School and that he was currently waiting for results from the California Bar Exam. Directly across from me was a relatively tall and solidly built guy named Kingcrey. He looked to be in good shape, said little, and was apparently looking forward to being recycled momentarily. It was also at this point that I met Dave Marshall. He stepped forward, stuck out his hand and said, "Daley, I'm Dave Marshall. I was in the 49th OC before I fractured my kneecap."

Marshall was a few inches taller than me with closely-cut blonde hair and a thin and gangly build. Dave was from Dallas, Texas, but, to my New York ears, seem to have only a very slight accent. He had a quick and contagious laugh and a "salty" manner about him. One thing I would learn about Marshall later on was that he was always listening and always thinking. He was most assuredly no Texas hick. Another Texan with Marshall was from Lubbock and I simply could not understand a word that he was saying. His drawl was simply too heavy.

Marshall introduced him as Butts. I found the contrast between these two individuals from Texas, both in mannerisms and speech, to be startling. So much for stereotypes! Doug Vredeveld was a quiet guy from Michigan who said little and very seldom went out with the other guys. Over the next month or so guys would come and go but eventually there would develop a core contingent that would include Marshall, myself, Vredeveld, Al Dank from New York, Tommy Hinkle from Philadelphia, and John Cullen from Fort Smith, Arkansas. It would take me a few weeks but eventually I would get a handle on all the wrinkles involved in Casual Company and what you wanted to do and what you didn't want to do.

All of us in Casual were classified as "TNPQ" or temporarily not physically qualified. What you really wanted to be, I would soon learn, was "NPQ" or not physically qualified. When you were classified as "NPQ" that meant that you were going home. You were out of the Marine Corps. Getting classified as "NPQ" in the Marine Corps was hard enough but with the Viet Nam War raging and both the military and politicians traumatized by the very recent Tet Offensive, it became harder yet. The Marine Corps was not looking to let go of anyone, not if they could possibly help it.

Periodically, those in Casual Company were subject to medical reevaluations or what were simply referred to as "Re-Evals." My short leg cast was scheduled to come off in three weeks and, coincidentally, that was the date of the next "Re-Evals." Robledo made it a point to wander around the squad bay singing new lyrics to the melody of an old song. The new lyrics were, "The security of a cast when Re-Evals come."

The old lyrics and melody were, "The shadow of her smile…"

At this point I hadn't fully figured out Robledo's scam, but I would after the next Re-Evals.

Even though we were in Casual Company and classified as "TNPQ" and hoping for "NPQ", we still had to roll out of the rack at 5:45 AM each morning. Whoever was on duty would flip on the lights in the squad bay and holler, "Reveille! Reveille! Get out of those racks."

Amidst grunts and groans, we would roll out, hit the head to shave, shower and shit and form up for whichever NCO was currently in charge. There was one notable exception to our morning routine in the form of Robledo who would quickly roll out of his rack and slide under his bunk for an extra ten minutes of snooze time until whoever was on duty walked thru to check the racks. Most everyone was now used to Robledo's antics and they would kick his rack and sound off, "Robledo! Get out from under that rack."

At that time, the NCOIC or Non-Commissioned Officer In Charge was Corporal Joe Biggers. Joe had been a teacher in South Carolina who had either enlisted or been drafted into the Marine Corps. He then had managed to make it into OCS. His injury consisted of a lacerated kidney which he incurred when he fell down the side of the trail on one of the forced marches. My first thought was he had experienced heat stroke and fainted. Biggers, however, would laugh and insist that he had whiskey in his canteen at the time and that had been the primary cause of his fall. Whether that was true or not was hard to tell but it made for a good story.

Joe was a relatively easygoing but large black man. He was a couple of inches over six foot with a pleasant though not particularly handsome face. During the riots in D.C. in '68, Biggers would brag about driving downtown to party with various girlfriends, both black and white, to hear him tell it, in spite of the chaos in the streets. He insisted that he would simply park his car and write "Soul Brother" on the windows with soap to prevent any marauding gangs from smashing the windows or torching it. Biggers' manner tended to make him seem like an unlikely candidate to be the "NCOIC" but he definitely had an intimidating presence that got your intention when necessary. He was clearly not crazy about the job as he waited to be recycled and it took him a few tries to get the hang of corralling some of the wily characters in Casual.

In the beginning, he would have everyone form up and call the roll. He would then dismiss the formation telling everyone not to disappear because he had some work details to fill. That was another demeaning aspect of Casual Company. Once you were in it, you were a candidate for every crappy detail that they had. As soon as we were dismissed, however, the group was up the stairs to the second deck, out the window to the fire escape, down the ladder and gone within seconds. Biggers would then walk into the squad bay to find it empty except for himself and those who were too banged up to be assigned to a work detail. He'd look around and then growl, "Are you shitting me? Wait until I catch up to those mothers."

Casual Company members, of course, would not be seen again until the evening. It took Biggers only one session like this to figure out that he had to assign people to work details at formation. Biggers really was a good guy and tried to treat everyone fairly. He recycled a few weeks later, was commissioned, and, late the following year, Marshall and I saw a story about him in one of the Marine Corps newsletters. Lieutenant Joe Biggers had been wounded in Viet Nam and there was a picture of five or six guys holding his stretcher up as a cable was used to haul him up to a helicopter that was taking him out of combat. Interestingly enough, all of the enlisted men holding the stretcher up were white.

On my first weekend in Casual Company I drew a liberty card on Friday afternoon and drove home to New York with the cast on my left foot and my crutches stowed in the back seat. When I pulled into the driveway, my parents were both surprised and happy to see me. My mother, seeing me hobble out of the car on one foot, yelled at my father, "Help him. He's hurt."

My dad started to hustle out the door but I waved him off, "I'm okay. I'm fine. I've got it covered."

That evening was one of pure peace and relaxation. I never thought it would feel so good to sit in my parents' living room, watching television and drinking a cold beer. After I had recounted all my adventures to them leading up to my current predicament, my mother confessed that she had been praying for weeks that I would break my leg and not end up in Viet Nam. My unspoken thoughts on the subject were succinct, "Thanks, Mom. I really needed that."

I did manage to contact a few old friends while I was home and regale them with exciting tales of my training experiences. They all appeared suitably impressed if not disbelieving of some of the more hard to fathom details. By late Sunday afternoon I was back on the road and headed south towards Quantico.

My first experience with "Re-Evals" came a few weeks after I arrived in Casual Company. We all had to report at the hospital. When my turn came, they removed the cast and my first impression was that the foot looked about the same as when they put the cast on. It was still swollen and discolored. I had never been convinced that a cast was the right treatment to start with since it wasn't broken. This only reconfirmed that opinion. Doctors, however, especially in the Marine Corps don't usually ask your advice about the correct treatment. The Navy doctor that examined my foot wore gold oak leaves on his collar. That rank was equivalent to a Major in the Marine Corps but he was a Lieutenant Commander in the Navy. His first comment, as he studied the swollen foot, however, made him "shit" in my book, "You've been keeping that foot down. You haven't been keeping it elevated. That's why it's still swollen."

The accusatory tone in his voice raised my temper in a hurry. It really would not have mattered to me if he had been a general, "You put my foot in a cast which meant I couldn't move it. It was a non-walking cast and I had to keep it down to walk around on crutches. How was I supposed to keep the foot elevated?"

He stared at me silently trying to determine if I was being insubordinate or not. I suppose he had probably seen his share of guys trying to stay in Casual as long as possible, Robledo probably among them, but I didn't know that then. He then turned to the nurse, "Put the foot in a soft walking cast. I want to see him again in two weeks."

From then on my recovery would go pretty quickly. I was still on crutches with the soft cast but now I could put some weight on it. I would eventually graduate to an Ace bandage and a cane, and, finally, just a pronounced limp. For all of a year, when I would get up in the morning, my heel would not touch the floor until I walked around for a while and I never did have the same range of mobility in the foot again.

Following "Re-Evals", Biggers, Kincrey, and some others were recycled and soon were back in training. The rest of us remained in Casual Company for the foreseeable future, still not sure where that future was taking us. The good news was that the time spent in Casual was still what they call "good time." It counted against a minimum of two-years on active duty for someone who was categorized as USMCR or United States Marine Corps Reserve as opposed to the regular Marine Corps, USMC. If you were ever unfortunate enough to be sent to the brig that was known as "bad time," it did not count against your enlistment. You had to make the time up. For that reason, and many other worse reasons, no one wanted to go to the brig.

Following my first rotation through the "Re-Eval" turn-style, I saw Robledo in the squad bay one afternoon, working hard on the new cast on his foot. He seemed to be cutting the front of the cast back a bit. My first reaction was that it must be too tight and it's chafing him. Then, suddenly it hit me, "The security of a cast when Re-Evals come."

He was making sure that the small broken bone in his foot didn't heal completely. Each time they would remove the cast and X-Ray the foot, they would find the bone not fully healed. That would lead to another cast. He was "playing for time."

He had been in Casual before I arrived and he would be there after I left, and, it was all "good time." Robledo was working hard on getting that "NPQ." I have to admit that I was astonished that he would go to such lengths but it sounded like he, as well as many others in Casual, clearly had a plan. It was definitely food for thought as I started what would prove to be a three-month stay in Casual Company.

CHAPTER SEVEN

THE MANY FACES OF CASUAL COMPANY

Following my weekend at home and my first experience with "Re-Evals" a few weeks later, I began to settle into the routine of Casual Company. There was always a formation in the morning followed by assignment to work details, if there were any. Otherwise, we were pretty much on our own to spend the day as we saw fit with liberty in the evenings. One day a week, usually Thursday, we would "field day" the squad bay. Beyond that we, were all waiting for our next "Re-Eval." There were also those working hard at converting their "TNPQ" into an "NPQ." Standard procedure in Casual Company was to remove the "candidate" name tags which had a white background and black lettering, from the front and back of our utility shirts and field jackets. Those of us who had come from civilian life to the program began to wear the rank of PFC on the collar of our utilities. It was our understanding, more or less by word of mouth, that this was the payroll rank of a candidate until commissioned. Those who had been in Casual long enough or had entered the program from the enlisted ranks wore whatever their current grade happened to be. One of the better things about Casual was that you continued to earn rank and time in grade, while you were there. By the time that Marshall and I left Casual Company, he was a Lance Corporal while I was still a PFC. It wasn't a terrible existence just a very boring, frustrating, and seemingly wasteful one.

In addition to Robledo, the budding lawyer from Stanford, and Dave Marshall, Casual Company had more than its fair share of "strange pussycats" during my tenure there. One of the most interesting was Al Dank. Al was a "Jerry Lewis lookalike" from the borough of Queens in New York City. He had been dropped from the program in the eighth week. According to Al, his platoon sergeant used to scream at him, "Look at this shit! I got Jerry Lewis in my platoon."

I used to kid him about being "the only Jewish Marine" in captivity. Later, when we had both been transferred to Camp Lejeune, Al advised that he had checked it out and there were in fact three Jewish Marines at Lejeune. To my mind, it wasn't a question of Jewish Marines being "undesirables" in the Marine Corps it was a question of their usually being too smart to ever get themselves into such a mess. Al was definitely an exception and he had certainly entered the Marine Corps the hard way. He had actually been in the Army for a brief period when they discovered that he had a metal pin in his leg from a traffic accident several years earlier. As a result, they gave him a medical discharge. Al went to the trouble of having surgery to remove the pin and then enlisted in the Marine Corps. You have to admit that's really doing it the hard way. Al had been dropped from the program in the eighth week after he had frozen on a sixty-foot ladder that was part of the "Confidence Course." He was frozen in place and couldn't go up and couldn't go down. A couple of guys had to go up and get him. He apparently was afraid of heights. On the other hand, he later revealed to me that he used to fly gliders in civilian life. Figure that one out. Maybe he was just blowing smoke up my ass about the gliders, but I don't think so.

And then there was Tommy Hinkle. Hinkle was from Philadelphia, the city of brotherly love. He turned up at Casual not too long after I did. He had been in either the 51st or 52nd OC and had been a reporter for The Philadelphia Inquirer before entering Marine Corps OCS. I suspect that, like most of us, he had been "standing in a draft" when he enlisted but who really knew. Hinkle had a tough guy manner about him but he was pretty skinny at the time and seemed to smoke incessantly. He also had owned and ridden a motorcycle when he was a civilian and really broke us all up as he regaled us with stories of how he would drink beer at one of the local bars and then go outside and try and ride his motorcycle home. Inevitably, he would fall off his cycle a few times before he gave up, went back in the bar, and his friends would take pity on him and drive him home. I have to admit that Tommy's tough guy manner always struck me as "more show than go." On the other hand, I was from New York and he was from "Philly" so my judgment was probably a bit colored to start with.

Joe Steigerwald had been a young cop in Baltimore who had found himself instantly classified as "draft bait" when he had decided to leave the force. He had dislocated his elbow badly in training and was still hoping for his "NPQ." His right arm looked like a limp piece of spaghetti and it appeared to be every bit as bad as that of the future lawyer from Stanford. Joe knew all the low rent places in Baltimore. Most were to be found on "B" Street, better known as "The Block." Baltimore Street was a string of cheap strip joints and Joe seemed to know them all as well as the nuances of "the trade." He used to explain it all to us quite carefully beforehand. If you went in a place and stayed awhile you had to buy a beer and that would cost you at least $2.50. This was at a time when a beer usually cost about $ .50 in most joints. The strippers would do their "workout" on a runway which was actually part of the bar and then come down to sit with the customers at the bar. According to Joe, these girls were also peddling sex which they would promptly deliver in the back room. If they asked you to buy them a drink, you always had to say, "Not right now but maybe later. But, stay here and talk to us for a while."

If you were foolish enough to buy them a drink it would be a champagne cocktail at $5.00 a throw. Joe was smooth as silk in handling the girls. One of our favorite places was "The 408 Club" where "Upside Down Lulu" used to do her act. The first time that I met Lulu she sidled up to the bar and shook my hand as she introduced herself. I then noticed that her hand was very wet, seemingly sweaty. I immediately thought of what Joe had said about the back room and I started looking around for the men's room, hoping to find a sink with running water and a bar of soap.

John R. Cullen, Jr. was one of the more interesting personalities that I would encounter in Casual Company. He was from Fort Smith, Arkansas and he arrived a few weeks after me. All six foot seven inches of him wearing a full leg cast on his right leg hobbled in one afternoon on crutches. John's style, more by design than anything else, was "down-home hokum", accent and all. Some of his more noteworthy phrases were, "Well, no shit, Robledo!"

Alternatively, he would occasionally alter that a bit to, "Are you shitting me or what?"

John had actually been a schoolteacher in Fort Smith as well as occasional musician. He claimed to have played bass with a group but they kept getting fired because they would get so drunk during their gigs. Once they were sufficiently drunk they would entertain the customer with such endearing lyrics as, "I saw her snatch…the suitcase from the bed."

Their gig also included such old favorites as, "The old gray hound let out a fuss when we nailed his balls to the side of the bus…. He's moving on."

Ultimately, as John described it, the piano player would get so drunk that he would fall off of his stool and that was usually the end of the gig. I had always wanted to learn how to play guitar and Cullen agreed to teach me. But, first, I had to find a guitar. The two of us went down to a pawn shop on 14th Street in D.C. in the spring of 1968. The rioting had been hot and heavy at that time, primarily because of the assassination of Martin Luther King. The shop still smelled of tear gas as John thumped in on his crutches and I limped in on my cane to inquire about a guitar. The owner initially wanted $50.00 but settled for $35.00. I suspect our appearance had something to do with it. He probably figured that we had been shot up in Nam. I'm also sure that he realized that business had not been so great and it wasn't likely to improve much in the near term. We were able to pick up a set of new strings and a book on chords in a nearby music store and we were on our way. For the next few weeks I drove the squad bay nuts by learning to play Bob Dylan's "Don't Think Twice" on the guitar. I had managed to pick up a portable stereo at the Commissary and I worked hard at driving the "lifers" crazy by playing Arlo Guthie's "Alice's Restaurant", not to mention Dylan's "Highway 61 Revisited" and a few albums by Buffy Saint

Marie and Joan Baez. We were definitely preaching revolution with our taste in music. Occasionally, Cullen would break us all up by imitating one of the religious shows on the radio back home in Arkansas. He used to imitate old Brother John. He would strum on the guitar and rock back and forth on his rack as if in a rocking chair and softly entreat listeners to send in money, "Brothers and sisters, this is old Brother John asking you to send in some of those love offerings. I know that the devil is whispering in your ear and telling you not to do it but don't you listen to him. You just send in them dollar bills and Jesus will bless you. And if you can send in a five or a ten or even a twenty dollar bill, Jesus will bless you even more. Don't you be listening to that old devil, brothers and sisters, you just listen to Brother John and send in those love offerings."

Cullen would strum a little more on the guitar and the squad bay would roll on the deck with laughter.

On those occasions when we had liberty we would head for either "Q" Town (Quantico) or D.C. As members of Casual Company we were still members of the program but they preferred that we not hang out at the candidate's club. Although we were now wearing enlisted insignias, technically, we were not supposed to go to the "1-2-3 club" for enlisted below the rank of Corporal. Accordingly, we were left to our own devices. I remember one time that we either wangled an invitation to or "crashed" a party in a brownstone in D.C. Cullen was hard to miss given his size and his crutches, and, with his gift of "southern gab" he thrilled all the girls with tales of how he had been shot up in Nam and won the Silver Star. He was really a piece of work. Serious injury very nearly became a reality as we left the party, all of us quite drunk, and

Cullen, wobbly on his crutches even under normal circumstances, kind of froze in the middle of a relatively busy side street almost getting nailed by passing traffic. That night I figured we were either going to the hospital or to jail as Cullen stood in the middle of the intersection shouting at the drivers, "Well, no shit Sherlock! Why don't you just run me down?"

I suspect that the fact that he looked so pitiful and helpless on those crutches was the only thing that saved us.

Although John took great pride in his height, he would break us up as he described his experience with the troop handlers in the program during rifle drill. Cullen's rifle, of course, barely reached his hip and he was easily three or four inches taller than the next tallest man. This, of course, offended the platoon sergeant, "Cullen, you bag of shit. You're too damned tall. You're messing up my platoon."

On one occasion, John was rendered almost speechless as we encountered a first lieutenant in the mess hall who was easily six foot nine inches tall. He towered over Cullen and was a foot broader in the shoulders. Cullen just got kind of wide-eyed and said, "That son of a bitch is a friggin giant! He's huge! On the other hand, I'm better looking."

Doug Vredeveld was sort of a nonentity in the squad bay as was Charles Lamb from Georgia. Doug would kind of come and go on his own and you never knew exactly what he was thinking at any given point in time. He would occasionally go to a flick with us but almost never to one of the clubs to drink beer. We all figured that Vredeveld stashed away a lot of money during his tour. Lamb was a soft-spoken southerner who always looked like he was trying to melt into the woodwork. He would hang around at the fringes of the group and listen very careful but never seemed to make any decisive statements one way or another. He did worry a lot about Parris Island but that was nothing new. We all did. He would kind of get you in a corner and say very softly, "Daley, what are you going to do if they "PQ" you? Are you going to recycle? If you don't, do you think they'll send you to Parris Island for basic? I've heard that they might start doing that."

The truth is we were all in the same spot. No one really knew for certain what would happen if you didn't recycle. The "word", until now had been that they had shipped everyone to Infantry Training Regiment, better known as "ITR". The training was conducted at Camp Geiger, kind of an annex to Camp Lejeune. There was also a rumor around, however, to the effect that the Marine Corps was getting a bit strapped for second lieutenants and a bit pissed off at candidates that had chosen to "drop on request." Nobody was absolutely certain as to whether the rules had changed or might change in the near future. The idea of getting shipped to Paris Island to redo basic training under reportedly worse conditions than Quantico was not appealing and tended to increase the "pucker factor." In those days, the Marine Corps was not big on what they describe in legal parlance as "informed consent." They preferred to treat us like mushrooms by keeping us in the dark and covering us with shit. So to a certain extent you were on your own. As Dave Marshall would put it when discussing the alternatives between recycling or dropping from the program, "You pays your money and you takes your chance."

As taciturn as he appeared to be, Dave had a real talent with words. He just wasn't one for letting anyone know what was on his mind. Still, you could tell that the wheels were always turning. He was always plotting and planning and figuring the odds. On the other hand, he was not one for tipping his hand too soon. Being from Dallas, he was kind of a big city guy from a country and western state. But, in this case, it seemed a certainty that he had already made up his mind to drop from the program. When I arrived on the scene, he had already been in the Marine Corps for about four months and I couldn't see him giving them three more years of his time and, possibly, all of his life if he were shipped to Nam. However he managed it, if you wanted the "real scoop" on something, you consulted with Marshall and he usually had the "straight skinny."

CHAPTER EIGHT

DECISION TIME

As we moved thru April into May, it became more apparent that the clock was still ticking for a number of us and we would all have to make some decisions soon. The next set of officer candidate programs was scheduled to begin in June and the odds were pretty good that Marshall, myself, Hinkle, Dank, Lamb, and Vredeveld would all be declared physically qualified by then. The ankle was still bothering me but most of the swelling had gone down. I still had limited motion in the foot and it was really stiff when I first got up in the mornings. If I were not declared physically qualified and recycled next time out, I could really be at risk if I decided against accepting a commission and the policy relative to Parris Island changed. It was definitely a careful balancing act. Robledo, Steigerwald, the lawyer from Stanford, and some of the other more seriously injured would probably draw a pass at the next "Re-Evals" and would keep working hard on their "NPQ." Long term, Cullen was not likely to draw an "NPQ" but he was still hurting pretty good and would probably not be ready for the next set of programs either. The real question was what to do and when to do it.

After giving it some deep thought I decided that, if at all possible, I wanted to make a decision sooner rather than later.

If I could get myself declared physically qualified, I'd have a better idea of what the Marine Corps planned to do with me. If I waited, they might change the rules and that would mean I'd have to recycle or face going to Parris Island. I personally didn't like the odds on the Marine Corps trying to "do the right thing" by me. I decided that my best bet was to push it a bit and try to get myself declared physically qualified. That would make the Marine Corps show its hand first with regard to how they planned to recycle me and I would then be in a better position to make a decision.

Coincidentally, long about the time that I was mulling all this over I happened to run into Puida. It was late on a Friday afternoon in May. I had already drawn a liberty card and we were both wearing civilian clothes. I literally almost ran into him on the sidewalk overlooking the parking lot behind our squad bay. There really was no way to avoid talking to him. He didn't look terribly comfortable with the situation either, but after glancing to his left and right quickly, he also realized that there was no easy avenue of escape. I led off, "Staff Sergeant, how are you doing?"

There was clearly no protocol for this kind of a situation and, with no place to run, he stood his ground as well, "Daley! You're still here? I thought for sure that you'd be gone by now."

I have to admit that I really wanted to stick it to him a bit so I kind of shrugged and said, "Well, the ankle's still bothering me a bit and I'm waiting to see if they're going to "PQ" me this time around. At some point I have to decide whether I want to take the commission or just go enlisted and go home in eighteen months."

Puida looked a little surprised at the tone that the conversation had taken, almost as if no one in his right mind would turn down the opportunity to get commissioned and he asked me quite earnestly, "What do you think you're going to do?"

I was actually being pretty straight with him in my answer, "I really don't know yet. I haven't decided. I'm not crazy about the idea of doing the first five weeks all over again but I'll have to wait and see how it goes."

I could see Puida mulling this over a bit and I almost sensed a little bit of embarrassment, almost shame on his part as he asked, "How far did you go in the program, Daley?"

I kind of studied him a bit, seeing a different side of him before answering, "Well, I finished five weeks. I got hurt in the sixth week on that admin move. I tore up my ankle pretty good."

He kind of nodded, "Yeah, I remember now. That foot was a mess. What happened? You stepped in a hole or something, didn't you?"

I thought about letting him off the hook right then and there but I couldn't quite bring myself to make it that easy for him, "No, actually, if you remember, we were double timing and I twisted my ankle with the field transport pack on. I guess it was just too much weight. It really tore the ankle up pretty good."

There was a moment of silence as we stared at one another. Neither one of us blinked but he finally offered, "You know, if you completed five weeks, they'll probably put you in the second half of the PLC (Platoon Leaders Class) program. That's really a pretty easy program compared to what you went through before. You know, it's all those college kids coming back for their second summer. You could probably breeze right through it."

At that I smiled, "You're probably right, Staff Sergeant. Thanks for the scoop."

We shook hands, wished each other luck, and turned to go, each of us heading in a different direction. It occurred to me just for a moment that each of us was uncomfortable in the presence of the other and was anxious to get away.

I remember that it was around that time that I called Sharon. Sharon was a stewardess with TWA and shared an apartment with a friend on East 18th Street in downtown Manhattan. She was vivacious and lively and always smiling. I had started seeing her after my engagement had broken up and just before I went into the Marine Corps. As a matter of fact, I took her home from my going-away party in Manhattan. We were both pretty drunk and she let me sleep over on her couch. She had an early flight the next morning and I was amazed at how good she looked grabbing a cab to the airport and how terrible I both looked and felt. Those stewardesses are really tough. I hadn't really been in touch with her since leaving for Quantico. I have to admit that right around that time I was really starting to waver about what to do in the future. Guys like Kincrey and Biggers were already back in training while I was still hanging around in Casual Company.

When Sharon answered the phone she really lifted my spirits off the floor, "Vince Daley! Where the hell have you been? I thought you were dead or something."

As high as she sounded I felt obligated to play along, "Sharon, yeah, I'm really sorry. I thought I was dead too but I was just in Casual Company for the last month or so."

I recapped my whole sad story for her, adding that I had even been back to New York at least once to see my folks, but she refused to let me dampen her spirits, "I can't believe that you were back in New York and you didn't call me. When are you going to be back in town again?"

I explained that I would have liberty over the upcoming weekend, and, fortunately for me, her flight schedule meshed with my travel plans. We agreed that I would meet her at her apartment on Saturday afternoon, as soon as I arrived.

On the drive up to New York, I thought about Sharon a lot. She was a year or two younger than I was and almost as tall. She was a lanky brunette who you wouldn't describe as pretty but rather as very attractive. She also always seemed to be smiling. Her build was that of an athlete, at a time when it hadn't yet become fashionable, with long legs, square shoulders, and small breasts. At first glance, she seemed tomboyish and almost awkward in her movements but she was a thoroughly upbeat and exciting woman. When we were first dating, she had invited me to visit her folks' home in Batavia, New York over a long weekend. At the time, I was trying hard not to get too involved with anyone and I declined. Although she smiled at my answer, I could see the hurt in her large brown eyes.

It was early afternoon when I arrived in New York and, fortunately, I was able to find a parking place a block away from her apartment that looked safe. In New York, even in those days, you never knew for sure if your car would still be there when you returned. If they didn't tow it, someone was likely to steal it. I was still hobbling around on my cane at that time and when Sharon answered the door to her apartment, her welcoming smile turned quickly to a look of concern as she noticed the cane and my pronounced limp. On the other hand, I noticed that she was dressed in a beautiful negligee. Automatically, we reached for each other and kissed warmly as if the intervening four months had never been. Perhaps sensing that I was reacting a little too warmly too quickly, she pushed me away, "Oh, no. First we eat. I didn't spend all morning cooking for nothing."

As I entered the apartment I could see that the table was set for dinner and a bottle of white wine was chilling on the table. I kicked myself for not thinking to bring wine but I'd have to find a way to make it up to her. We ate and drank, talked and laughed. And then we made love as I tried to remember why I had left Sharon and New York for the Marine Corps but no answers came readily to mind. We made love twice more that afternoon, each time a bit more gently than the previous effort, and then we dressed and made plans to go out for the evening.

We decided that we would go to "Your Father's Moustache" on 10th Street in the village. It was a sing-a-long place that served peanuts and beer while a musical group that included at least one banjo, a trombone, and a drummer, played medleys of old songs. I tried to leave the cane behind at the apartment but Sharon would have none of it, "Oh no you don't! You're supposed to use this thing. Don't you want to get better?"

My answer was in the form of a grimace that showed how much I wanted to "get better" and go back to the Marine Corps. In the few months that I had been away, long hair, sideburns, moustaches, and bell-bottom pants had hit the scene in New York. If I didn't feel conspicuous enough in chinos, a short-sleeve shirt, penny loafers, and a short haircut, the cane was definitely the icing on the cake. But, I did take the cane. It was dented and banged from my having used it for batting practice on soda cans and beer cans pitched to me in the parking lot at Quantico, but without it, my limp was atrocious.

As I had feared, our entrance at "Your Father's Moustache" drew some attention. For a moment, I thought the hostess was going to carry me to my table. We ordered a pitcher and I quickly downed a couple of beers and swallowed a few handfuls of peanuts, throwing the shells on the floor as instructed. It was only a question of time until they played a military medley that included the Marine Corps Hymn. When they did, as much as I hated to make more of spectacle of myself, I felt obligated to stand for that song. Perhaps I was just showing off. Who really knows what's in your mind when you're twenty-five years old and in the military at a time when the world keeps moving on as if everything is normal but it really isn't. As for Sharon, God bless her, she felt obligated to help as well. Amidst the applause of onlookers, she kept shouting, "Marines! Marines!"

And I continued to wonder what planet we all were on. Years later, I think back on that moment and the insanity of the times. Men were dying in Viet Nam at a record pace while civilians were drinking beer, eating peanuts, and singing happy songs. And as for me, I wasn't sure where I stood. What did I feel? Did I feel patriotic? Did I feel proud? Did I feel like a fraud? Did I feel like I was in love with Sharon at that moment or did I only feel pity for myself? It had been a wonderful weekend but all too soon I was on my way back to Quantico, returning to a life that I didn't even understand anymore. I'd been confused when I left on liberty and, now, upon my return, I found myself wavering about whether I should simply recycle and accept the commission. Both time and my options were running out. But, I did return with a plan. I had decided to get myself designated as physically qualified "by hook or by crook" and then wait to see what my orders relative to recycling looked like. If they assigned me to the second half of the PLC program I'd probably go ahead and take the commission. If they recycled me back through the entire ten weeks of the program, I was done. I would "D.O.R." and take my chances with Parris Island.

When I shared my thoughts with Dave Marshall he was decidedly unimpressed, "You're nuts, Daley. You go to New York to see your girlfriend, have a great weekend, and then you come back here and tell me that you might want to recycle? After New York I figured you'd be so pissed off at the Marine Corps that you might not come back at all. Recycle! Ha! That'll be the day."

I pleaded my case halfheartedly, "Well, I just want to keep my options open. If it's only six weeks in the PLC program, I might want to do it."

Marshall was not to be persuaded, "You do what you want but I'm telling you that I don't plan to give the Marine Corps fifteen minutes longer than I have to. They haven't done me any favors lately or, for that matter, ever. And, I don't plan to wait around to see if they're going to change the rules about

Parris Island. Even if they do, the way I figure it, it's still eighteen months and a wakeup. I'm going to do my year and a half and then I'm going home. After that I don't want to hear anything from anybody about anything. I'm going to do what I want and say what I want. Here's to the Marine Corps: "Ra ha tooey!"

This was probably more than I had ever heard Marshall say about anything. He was usually not one to share his thoughts with anyone about anything and these were particularly strong thoughts. He had been injured in the eighth week of the program and he was virtually "a lock" to get a slot in the PLC program. In my case, it was still "up for grabs." We did, however, agree on one thing. We both planned to get ourselves designated as physically qualified and we both planned to start running again. Whether it was going to be Parris Island, ITR, or back to the program, we would have to be in shape.

CHAPTER NINE

ON THE ROAD TO CAMP LEJEUNE

During the next few weeks, Marshall and I started running the trails in and around Quantico.

It was amazingly easy given that we were only wearing shorts, a sweatshirt and a soft cover. We did however run in boots. It was a far cry from running the trails with a rifle and a full load of equipment during the dead of winter. Surprisingly, we were both still in pretty good shape and the runs were manageable. The ankle was still bothersome when I first got up in the morning or when we first started to run but as we continued it began to loosen up considerably. I was still a bit concerned about getting myself "PQ'd", but I was determined not to waste any more time in Casual Company. If I didn't get myself ready in the next few weeks there was no way that I would have a chance at the PLC program. The flip side of that was if I didn't make the PLC program and I "dropped on request", the longer that I waited, the greater the chance that Parris Island could become a part of my future. As bad as the first six weeks of Quantico had been, I had no doubt that Parris Island would be worse, particularly, for someone who had consciously turned down another shot at OCS. It was not a theory that I wanted to test if there was any way to avoid it.

Fairly quickly, the word had gotten around the squad bay that Marshall and I were working on making some kind of move in the very near future. Robledo and some of the others who were working hard on their "NPQ" thought we were absolutely nuts, "Are you crazy? Just wait them out. Tell them your ankle still hurts. You can't walk on it, much less, run on it. Wait them out. I've seen you get out of the rack in the morning. That ankle is still screwed up. You can beat this."

On the other hand, Tommy Hinkle, also figuring the odds wanted in, "I hear that you guys are going to D.O.R. What about Parris Island? You think they've changed that yet? You could get shipped there. I don't know what I want to do yet but let me know when you're going to make your move. "

Hinkle had a good point. We were definitely pushing the envelope and, if we got hit with it, Parris Island would be a real bitch. Marshall wasn't buying it, but, either way, he was going for it, "The word that I have is that they haven't changed the rule yet but they might real soon. I ain't waiting around to see if they do. If they get us, they get us. Either way, we go home early."

The next "Re-Evals" were scheduled for early June but I wanted to have as much time to work with as possible. I already had an appointment to see the doctor towards the end of May, about two weeks before the next "Re-Evals." Ever since my first visit when the doctor complained about the swelling in the foot and "not keeping the foot elevated", they had been keeping pretty close tabs on me. I would trek down to the hospital every two weeks or so for ongoing observation and evaluation. You really had to laugh about it. Here they were monitoring me when all I wanted was to get the hell out of Casual Company. Meanwhile, Robledo and a few others were making a career out of being "TNPQ" with high hopes of reaching the big "NPQ in the Sky."

The Navy doctor at the hospital studied my foot thoughtfully and nodded, "That foot's really starting to come along pretty well. There's still some lack of motion but most of the swellings gone. How's the pain?"

I casually lied through my teeth, "No real pain at all, sir. I get a twinge every now and again but nothing to speak of."

The doctor looked pleased with himself, "Okay, Daley. Sounds good! I think I'm scheduled to see you in a couple of weeks in any event. Maybe, we can get you "PQ'd" then."

I could sense him studying me for some reaction to the idea of being designated physically qualified in the near term, "That sounds good, sir. But, I was wondering if it would be possible to push that schedule up a bit. I was wondering if you could "PQ' me now and save us both having to go through this all over again in a couple of weeks?"

I almost regretted laying it out there that quickly because he hesitated, looked at me again, and I could see the wheels turning in his head, "What is this guy up to? What have I missed?"

But he swallowed all his thoughts but one, "What's the big hurry? That ankle's looking better. In two weeks it will be better yet. Maybe you should give it a little more time."

One of life's lessons to me has been that whenever someone says "To tell you the truth", they aren't telling you the truth. Still, I pushed on with it, "To tell you the truth, sir, I've been stuck in Casual Company for over two months and I'd like to get my life going again. I'm sure my ankle might be a little better in two weeks but it's pretty good now. I don't think it's going to get worse. Why not just get it over with now?"

My explanation was certainly plausible but I could tell that he still wasn't really buying it. Nobody in his experience had ever pushed for a "PQ" and an out from Casual Company. He knew that I had something working but at the same time I could see the resignation set in his face. Either way, he really didn't give a shit. It wasn't his problem, "To designate you physically qualified I have to check the ankle out a little more closely."

I nodded my understanding, "Thank you, sir."

For the next fifteen minutes he prodded and poked and twisted the foot back and forth and up and down, always watching me closely. Then we came to the moment of truth, "I want you to stand on the bad foot, lift your other foot and keep jumping up and down."

I gritted my teeth and did so, hoping not to emit any sounds of pain. After half a dozen hops, he asked, "How's that feel? Is there any pain?"

I'm sure he could see it all in my eyes but screw him. I answered decisively, "No Sir. There's no pain. No pain at all."

Again, he studied me silently for a moment before saying, "Okay, the foot's fine. As of now you're physically qualified. Good luck."

I often wondered whether he made me hop up and down like that to really test how the good the foot was or just to make me pay the full price in pain for my request. It really didn't matter to me. I had my physically qualified designation and, for better or worse, I would soon be on my way.

By the end of the first week in June, the latest "Re-Evals" were over and, as expected, in addition to Marshall and myself, Tommy Hinkle, Al Dank, Doug Vredeveld, and Charles Lamb had all been reclassified as physically qualified to be recycled. Robledo, the lawyer from Stanford, Joe Steigerwald, and John Cullen, as well as a host of others, remained "TNPQ." Within a week, we would all receive our orders relative to the recycle. Decision time was most assuredly upon us as we all waited for the other shoe to drop. Marshall remained adamant that he did not plan to take a commission even if they made him a general. My plan remained about the same while the others watched each other warily while waiting and hoping for some sort of divine enlightenment or divine intervention. When the orders finally came through Marshall and all the others had been assigned to the second half of the PLC program at the Annex while I drew "D" Company. That meant that they were recycling me for the full ten weeks or so they thought at the time. From my perspective, that was really the "last straw." In truth, it was only four additional weeks of training time over and above the PLC program but the Marine Corps once again had managed to "add insult to injury." They had poured salt in the wound and I'd had enough. The decision had been taken out of my hands and my thoughts that day definitely ran to the dark side, "Fuck the Marine Corps. I can't believe that I was so stupid as to even consider recycling under any circumstances. I don't give a shit if they ship me to Parris Island and then to Viet Nam. However you slice it, I'm going home in a year and a half."

The Marine Corps had done nothing but fuck me around for the past five months and I'd had my fill. The party was over. Marshall and I marched into battalion headquarters almost before the ink was dry on our orders to advise them that we were not going to recycle. We were going to "D.O.R." The "Gunny" on duty looked a little surprised at our alacrity but merely nodded, drew up the necessary forms, and we signed them. Neither one of us even asked about whether they were going to ship us to Parris Island or Camp Geiger for ITR. The "Gunny" then gave me one additional piece of information, "Daley, your service record book is still down at "E" Company headquarters at the Annex. You'll need it in order to check out of here and to check in at your next duty station. You want me to send down for it or do you want to go pick it up yourself? Don't know if you're in a big hurry or not but it might save some time if you did it."

It occurred to me that the sooner we were out of here the better, particularly, if they were contemplating changing the rules. I almost had the feeling that the "Gunny" was trying to tell me something. I also wondered why my SRB was still at "E" Company after so many months, "I'll get it Gunny and drop it off here later today. Thanks for the heads up."

Marshall rode down to the Annex with me but waited in the car. I soon found myself entering "E" Company headquarters and lots of bad feelings started to wash over me as I entered the low block-style building. I thought to myself, "Take it easy. You're probably just revisiting some bad memories."

But, my gloomy feelings had been on target. The duty officer was the XO, Captain Mahoney, the king-sized prick who had stood over me and taunted me when I went down with the field transport pack on my back. I came to attention and spoke with no hesitation. I'd come a long way in the last five months and this guy no longer impressed me, "Sir, I'm Candidate Daley and battalion headquarters asked me to come down here and pick up my SRB. I've been in Casual Company since March and I understand that it's still here, sir."

Mahoney waited a second or two before looking up. Still playing his fucking games I thought to myself. If he remembered me he gave no hint of it, "Why do you need your SRB, Daley?"

I really enjoyed the next part, "I've just dropped on request from the program, sir."

He looked curious now, "You sure that's what you want to do?"

My response was almost instantaneous, "Yes sir. I'm sure. No doubt about it."

Mahoney pulled the book from the files and glanced at it, "You're the guy that stepped in a hole and tore up his ankle, aren't you?"

He glanced at me across the desk, "No, sir. Actually, we were double-timing with a field transport pack on and I turned my ankle."

Mahoney glanced at the record again, "That's not what it says here. It says you stepped in a hole while you were marching on an admin move."

The abruptness of my answer must have caught him off guard, "Then it's wrong sir. I didn't step in a hole. We were double-timing, I twisted my ankle, and the weight of the pack took me down and tore up the ankle."

Now I could see that this was clearly going to be a case of stonewalling, "Well, Daley. I don't know how you're going to get this record changed now. It's already been entered and signed off on. Nothing I can do about it."

I guess he was expecting a more contentious answer but I was already well past that, "Actually, sir, I don't care if they change it or not now. I'm out of the program. I just want to get my records and get going."

I'm sure Mahoney was still wondering if I was trying to set him up or not but I really wasn't. It didn't surprise me that they had recorded the incident the way they had. What else could Puida do? He couldn't admit to violating regulations and getting a man injured as a result. No way was he going to do that. And the truth was I really didn't give shit at this stage of the game.

Mahoney drew up a receipt for the SRB. I signed it and I headed back to the car. Seeing the grim set to my face Marshall asked, "How'd it go? Everything's alright?"

I kind of smirked as I started the car, "No problem. That scumbag, Mahoney, the "XO", was the duty officer. All they did was lie their asses off about how I got hurt and that's the way it got recorded in my SRB."

Marshall just kind of grinned, "Well, no shit Daley! Did you think they were going to tell the truth and put their own asses in a sling? I figured that from the beginning. Who gives a shit? Let them play their games. Soon, it will all be over."

Word had traveled fast through the squad bay about Marshall and I having dropped from the program and now everyone was waiting to see how it turned out. They wanted to see where the Marine Corps shipped us. We were going to be the guinea pigs. To his credit, Hinkle had decided not to wait either. He was about a day behind us in tendering his "D.O.R."

When the orders finally did come through a few days later there was a collective sigh of relief. Marshall, Hinkle and I had been ordered to report to MCB, Camp Lejeune no later than June 20, 1968 for "further assignment and training." Presumably, that meant ITR. At least it wasn't Parris Island. That was also the "go signal" for Dank, Vredeveld, and Lamb to submit their "D.O.R.'s."

As is the way of such things, we decided that a little party was in order before Marshall, Hinkle and I shoved off. Joining us in this undertaking was the pride of Fort Smith, Arkansas, John R. Cullen, Jr. We also decided that, on such an auspicious occasion and in light of the fact that we were soon to join the ranks of enlisted personnel, our going away shindig should be held at the "1-2-3 Club." The fact that Cullen was still on crutches and easy to pick out in a crowd may have put our endeavor at risk but we were not to be dissuaded. We were all dressed in suits and ties when I drove down to the club to begin a lengthy evening of drinking in celebration of the shaking off of the dust of Quantico from our collective heels. Cullen was not physically able yet to accompany us to Camp Lejeune and what lay beyond but, even though "his flesh was weak, his spirit was not." He got the drunkest in the shortest period of time, with the possible exception of Tommy Hinkle. The pitchers of beer flowed freely and just as we all began to feel thoroughly mellow, trouble reared its ugly head.

At a nearby table sat a very attractive female who also happened to be a lance corporal in the Marine Corps. Broad Ass Marines or "BAMs", for the most part, are all "sister uglies" but this one was not. We had all seen her around the base and she was definitely well put together. That, of course, led to some serious ogling on our part. The four or five other Marines at the table, including the guy she was with, ultimately took offense and decided to have a word with us about it. Her boyfriend spoke first in a deep southern accent, "You guys better quit staring at my girl like she's some sort of whore."

Finding myself more sober than my compatriots I tried to make peace lest we find ourselves on the inside of the brig looking out, "Hey, man. We're sorry about that. We didn't mean to make her feel uncomfortable. No problem. We'll be hitting the road soon anyhow."

But he was not so easily put off, "You guys ain't even supposed to be in here. So just quit it or I'm going to come over here and kick your ass."

That was a serious mistake on his part. This guy stood perhaps a shade under six feet. At these last words, Cullen, still leaning on his crutches for balance, stood up to his full six feet seven inches, "Are you shitting me or what? You're going to kick my ass? You're a fucking midget next to me."

Marshall had also stood with an empty pitcher in his hand and was looking for swinging room, "Get out of the way, Daley! I'll take care of this sucker."

I grabbed Dave and pushed him back while Hinkle, the only one still sitting, also chimed in, "Tell these guys to fuck off. We're having a party here."

Suddenly there were chairs, tables, and pitchers flying as Hinkle and I hustled Cullen towards the door. This was definitely not the place to be. Somehow, Marshall disappeared in the melee. We waited in the car outside for at least ten or fifteen minutes but Marshall was a no show. We didn't even see him on a slow ride back to the squad bay. It had to be slow because we were all pretty drunk. My biggest hope was that they hadn't picked up Marshall and that no one in the place had been able to clearly "ID" any of us, at least until after we had gotten out of town. The next morning we found Marshall sleeping peacefully in his rack with his suit in a wet pile on the floor next to him. When we asked him what had happened to him and how he had gotten back or how he had gotten so wet, he couldn't seem to recall, "Beats the shit out of me. I just headed for the door of the club and kept on trucking. I remember something about water but I can't quite get a handle on it. Maybe, I fell in the creek or something on the way back."

We spent the rest of the day waiting for the military police ("The P.'s") to show and pick us up but, somehow, we had managed to skate out of it. Marshall, Hinkle and I did not waste any more time saying "sad good byes." We simply packed and started making tracks. We weren't too worried about Cullen. We doubted that they would throw a guy on crutches in the brig even if they did track him down. Hinkle, Marshall and I headed out early the next morning and drove south on 95 past Richmond. Surprisingly, Richmond was kind of an ugly town, at least looking at it from the highway in passing. It was kind of a cluster of gray and grimy buildings packed closely together. Not really a great advertising poster for the "new south." We passed Petersburg and kept heading south until we crossed the state line and entered North Carolina. We continued south for perhaps another hour before turning east. We had all dressed in civilian clothes and we planned to change into our uniforms before reporting in at Lejeune. Whatever doubts I had about this decision, I tried to put them out of my mind as I drove. All I wanted to do was get started again, moving in some specific direction and in a year and a half I planned to be back in New York. Hinkle seemed to be the most nervous of the three of us. He really did not want to go thru any more training, if there was any way of avoiding it. He was also a little nervous about joining the "regular troops." Up until now we had all had it tough, physically, at Quantico but the guys we had trained with all had their "heads and asses wired together." Now we were going to get a chance to see some of those "good old boys" that the Marine Corps had a talent for attracting. It was tough to tell what lay ahead in ITR but it was definitely on Hinkle's mind, "Listen, I really don't want to go through ITR. When we check in we've got to tell them that they told us we would be assigned an MOS and given a job at Lejeune. We just have to tell them that nobody ever mentioned ITR to us."

Marshall said nothing but I suspected that his thoughts were the same as mine. There was no way that we were going to avoid ITR. We were lucky to have "skated" on Parris Island. Both Hinkle and Marshall had gone into the eighth week in the program before getting shuttled to Casual Company and I could see why they might not want to do an additional three weeks of any kind of training. In my case I had only gone into the sixth week before getting hurt so an additional three weeks didn't bother me all that much. As long as it wasn't Parris Island and it was all "good time", I'd be three weeks closer to going home when we finished up. My response was short and sweet, "Well, we can ask but my bet is that we're going to have to do it."

Hinkle became more agitated at my answer, "We just have to tell them that we're not supposed to go thru ITR. Nobody told us anything about ITR."

Marshall and I just glanced at each other. I had the feeling that Hinkle was starting to believe his own words. I guess he thought that if you said something enough times it eventually became true. It was becoming increasingly clear that Hinkle was going to be a real "Shaky Jake" in this deal. I really hoped that he would be up to handling it all.

As we drove east into North Carolina and towards the coast, the differences between Virginia and East Carolina became more apparent. The country seemed to be more barren, if anything. The soil looked sandy and the trees and grass looked scraggly. Next to the small two-lane roads that we traveled as we moved east were shacks with peeling paint or no paint at all that were precariously balanced on cinder blocks. In some cases the houses canted downward at one end or the other. Outside the shacks poorly dressed black children played and looked up curiously as our car passed by. The level of poverty was disturbing and it was hard to believe that we were still traveling in America. At one point on one of those lonely two-lane roads we encountered a large billboard sign that proudly proclaimed, "You are now entering Klan country."

That sign quickly got all of our attention. Hinkle was clearly shocked, "Holy shit! Did you see that sign? What the hell kind of place is this? Don't stop for nothing man. Just keep on moving."

Even though he was a big city boy from Dallas, being from Texas, Marshall had obviously seen stuff like this before and felt obligated to chip in his two-cents worth, "You're in redneck country now, boys. We ain't in downtown Philly or New York City. These boys down here are the real deal. You get crossways of them and you'll wish you hadn't."

As we trucked along in my two-year old Plymouth Sport Fury with New York State license plates on it, I thought about the three civil rights workers that were killed in Mississippi in my sophomore year at Fordham. One of them had come from Pelham Parkway, right down the street from Rose Hill Campus. This looked like serious stuff and I sure didn't plan on becoming a statistic during my brief sojourn in the "good old south."

The ride from Quantico to Jacksonville, North Carolina, a small town just outside the gates of Camp Lejeune was all of six hours with at least one stop along the way. Whatever negative thoughts I had about the small town quality of Quantico were quickly displaced by my first exposure to Jacksonville. The town was a small strip of beer joints and a few small stores, not to mention, a gas station or two. This town looked like the armpit of the world. Suddenly, those "eighteen months and a wakeup" were looking longer and longer. We pulled into the closest gas station, filled the tank, and took turns changing into our uniforms in the men's room. One thing about wearing a uniform is that you feel immediately vulnerable to anyone who wants to give you a "ration" of shit, particularly if you are standing in the shadows of a large military base, like Camp Lejeune. During the next eighteen months, whenever I traveled home on liberty, I would never wear my uniform unless I was flying, and then, only to get a discount on the ticket. On one occasion in early 1969, I remember seeing some "brown bar" a Marine Corps "boot lieutenant" jerking two Army guys around in LaGuardia airport because he didn't think that they looked squared away. I had quickly stepped outside the main lobby of the airport terminal in order to put some distance between myself and this "jerkoff lieutenant", and in the process, almost ran into a well-decorated green beret first lieutenant with a tall leggy woman on his arm. He was built like a fireplug and was easily a good four inches shorter than she was. Almost without thinking, I snapped to attention and saluted but he just smiled and waved me off. You gotta love a guy like that. He had clearly been "in the shit" but he wasn't going to waste his time jerking around some enlisted guy, especially with a woman like that on his arm. He had "places to go and things to do."

Once we had changed into our uniforms, I could even sense a change in the attitude of the guy pumping gas for the car. One minute you were a reasonably well-dressed civilian driving a nice car and the next you were just another "dipshit" marine in a town full of "dipshit" marines. The change in attitude was palpable.

The sign at the main gate proclaimed our arrival at Camp Lejeune, North Carolina, home of the 2nd Marine Division. Just for a moment, it occurred to me that the sign would have been more appropriate had it read, "Abandon all hope ye that enter here."

I quickly dismissed that fleeting thought, not realizing at the time, how prophetic it would prove to be.

CHAPTER TEN

WE'RE NOT SUPPOSED TO GO THRU ITR

After passing thru the main gate of Lejeune and stopping to get a parking pass, we headed for the personnel office. Almost before the car had started moving again, Hinkle was chirping away, "Remember now, we have to tell them. No ITR. No matter what they say. We have to be tough."

Marshall and I said nothing.

Interestingly enough, the person checking us in at the personnel office was a seemingly nice middle-aged lady rather than the tough First Sergeant or Gunny that we were expecting to see. As we handed her our orders and our SRB'S, I noticed that Hinkle immediately lapsed into silence and stood behind Marshall and myself. Although I considered it a lost cause, I thought that I should at least take a shot at the "no ITR pitch". Feeling a little foolish, I put on my most sincere face and asked politely, "Excuse me ma'am, but do you know where we're going to be assigned? They said something to us at Quantico about getting an MOS at Camp Lejeune and then being given an assignment."

She studied our orders and glanced at our SRB's before answering in a soft southern accent, "Well, according to this, you guys have to go through ITR before they can assign you an MOS."

Neither Marshall or Hinkle spoke but we all tried to look suitably perplexed and murmured amongst ourselves before I responded, "Are you sure? I don't recall them saying anything about ITR when we left Quantico."

She was very nice about it but I could see her smiling to herself a bit. I had the feeling that she had heard all this before, "Yes, I'm sure. If you don't go thru ITR they won't assign you an MOS. There's a new class starting tomorrow. You can check in at Service Company for tonight. Just follow the signs. Come back here first thing tomorrow morning for your orders."

I glanced back at Hinkle who looked crestfallen but Marshall deadpanned it as usual, "Thank you ma'am. We'll see you in the morning."

She smiled an understanding good bye as if to say, "Nice try and no hard feelings."

We found our way to the Service Company Office and the company clerk checked us in drew some linen for us, and escorted us to a second-deck squad bay that appeared to be pretty empty, especially at that time of day. Later that afternoon a few of our fellow residents started drifting in and it was then that we got our first look at the "face of war." They were all young, certainly no more than eighteen or twenty years of age and, based on their accents, they appeared to be country boys, for the most part. I guessed Kentucky, West Virginia and perhaps a few other states. Many of them limped.

One kid had his leg bowed out like a boomerang from the knee to the ankle. As a few of them stripped off their utility shirts to hit the showers, we could see the scars on arms and chests. For those who had been hit in the chest, the wound on the chest was about the size of a nickel or a quarter but on their backs where the round had exited there was a patch of scar tissue that was easily four inches across. They were all "grunts" who had been wounded in action and shipped to the states to recover. They were now on "medical hold" either waiting to be discharged or reassigned. In the meantime, while they waited, they had been assigned some of the worst jobs in the Marine Corps. Usually it was to the "police gang." Their assignment was to clean buildings and police grounds on the base. This was certainly not a very glorious end for these young and bloodied combat veterans and I took careful note of how the Marine Corps appeared to "take care of its own." Marshall remained poker-faced but Hinkle's was ashen at the sight of the wounded. I could almost read Marshall's thoughts as well, "These guys have fought for their country, been wounded in action and, now, look at how they are being treated. It was just one more reason to go home early."

That evening, we located the mess hall, grabbed chow and wandered around a bit before hitting the rack. None of us really felt like drinking a few beers since our days would be pretty full beginning tomorrow and for the next twenty days or so. At 5:45 the next morning the duty clerk at Service Company rousted us from our racks by flipping on the lights and sounding off, "Reveille! Reveille! Get out of those racks."

One of the more obvious differences between Virginia and North Carolina, particularly East Carolina, was the climate. We were now well into June and the air hung over you like a wet blanket. There was no air conditioning and you found yourself waking up in a pool of sweat, even with all the windows in the squad bay "half-masted" as they liked to say. There was a kind of heavy smell in the area that reminded you of the damp and moldy smell of Florida airports, though not quite as strong. After showering and shaving, we dressed in starched utilities and starched covers and grabbed some chow. None of us was really all that hungry but the day ahead promised to be a long one so we made it a point to put away, eggs, toast, cereal and coffee. Although the food wasn't all that bad, it clearly was not as good as it was at Quantico. The food at OCS was exceptional even if they never gave you enough time to eat it. Whatever happened to the idea of "taking care of the troops first" I wondered? The three of us then trekked back over to the personnel office to pick up our orders and SRB's and that's when Hinkle's day went south in a hurry. Marshall and I had been assigned to the same training company in ITR but Hinkle had been assigned to a different one. That possibility had never occurred to any of us.

When Hinkle saw that we were in "M" Company and he was in "O" Company, I thought he would have a stroke right on the spot, "Holy shit! Son of a bitch! Give me a break! Why am I in a different company?"

Hinkle was really panicking now and, cruel as it was under the circumstances I still couldn't resist, "Well, maybe they heard that you were from Philly?"

I thought that Hinkle was going to start frothing at the mouth at any moment he was so beside himself, "Don't give me that shit. You're from New York. Why me?"

Of course Marshall felt obligated to pull his chain a bit as well, "Well, down here they don't much like Yankees in general but New York is still New York. It's kind of special. But Philly, on the other hand, ain't so special."

Marshall and I were both chuckling by the time that he finished that little discourse but Hinkle was in no mood, "Hey, fuck you guys. Give me a break. Here I am in "the armpit of the world" and I get to go it alone, while you two get to hang together. I should have stayed at Quantico."

We got some directions at the gate and we headed out towards Camp Geiger where Infantry Training Regiment was located. The drive over was not reassuring. Hinkle was right about one thing, though, this place really was "the armpit of the world." Geiger, if anything was a smaller, sparser version of Camp Lejeune. In fact, it made Camp Lejeune look pretty damn good. The squad bays were low slung depressing looking brick buildings. Across the road from each squad bay was another smaller low slung looking building. We would learn later that these were the showers. At the end of each training day we would strip down, put on our marine-green rain coats, shower clogs, and a soft cover to walk across the street to a shower. It looked like a "flasher's convention" and the water was almost always cold. We had thought that Lejeune was bad as compared to Quantico but, Camp Geiger, that was a real awakening. The living conditions in the squad bays were miserable and the food, seemingly always in short supply, was horrible. Fortunately or unfortunately, however you wanted to look at it, we would spend most of our days out in the field for the next three weeks so the condition of the squad bay and showers and the quality of the chow at the mess hall wouldn't prove to be all that relevant. We located "O" Company and dropped Hinkle off first. He appeared to still be in shock at the sight of the place and, accordingly, was less focused on having to go it alone for the next few weeks. Still he couldn't resist a parting shot, "Man, I don't believe this fucking place. I'll see you guys in a few weeks, if I live that long."

He wasn't smiling as he exited the car, grabbed his sea bag and headed towards the company office.

Following various posted signs, I drove towards the "M" Company area. We stopped at the company office but found it empty. Marshall and I wandered down the row of nearby buildings, finding all the squad bays empty except the last. Here we encountered a few live bodies. According to the occupants, the company was already out in the field. The three remaining individuals apparently had some sort of problem, either medical or administrative. One fellow with dark closely cropped hair sat on his footlocker brush shining a pair of field boots. A second individual with somewhat lighter colored complexion and hair and a nervous manner hovered close by. The third warm body, a grubby looking individual who appeared to be barely in shape judging by his rotund build, wore dirty and wrinkled utilities and appeared to be working hard at making himself look busy. It hadn't occurred to me until that moment that Marshall and I in our starched utilities and covers and shined field boots looked like troop handlers. The only thing that gave us away was our rank. Marshall wore the single stripe and cross rifles of a lance corporal on his collar while I wore the single stripe of a PFC. I spoke to the fellow shining his boots, "When's the company due back?"

He glanced at us casually, probably having figured out that we weren't there to hassle them, "Not really sure. Could be any time now. They headed out this morning. I had to get some shots, Davis here had to try and straighten out some paperwork, and Slotsky, down the end, is on sick call."

He looked us over carefully, "You guys joining the company?"

I nodded and added, "We're OC drops. We're here to go thru ITR. I'm Vince Daley and this is Dave Marshall."

The fellow shining his shoes studied me and asked, "Where you from?"

His accent sounded like the Northeast, maybe New York, "I'm from New York, out on the Island."

His eyes showed a glint of recognition, "Me too. You got a brother named, Paul?"

I hesitated before answering. My brother Paul had been in the Marine Corps for a little over a year and he seemed to have a habit of finding trouble. I hoped this wasn't someone that he had gotten crossways of, "Yeah, as a matter of fact I do. He's in the Marine Corps too. Last I heard he was out on the coast. You know him?"

He still hadn't smiled and I was getting a bit worried, "I know him. We went to school together. My name's Curran. You look like him."

This part surprised me a bit, "You went to high school with him? What the hell are you doing here?"

Curran grimaced before answering, "I went to college for a while but I kind of screwed that up. Next thing I know I'm getting drafted."

I still hadn't put it together, "You were getting drafted so you joined the Marine Corps?"

Curran looked at me like I had lost my mind, "Are you kidding me? They drafted me into the Marine Corps. They were so hard up for recruits that they were taking every fifth or sixth guy into the Corps."

The look on my face must have said it all, "Don't believe me? Ask Davis? He's there trying to talk them out of drafting him because he's married and he's going to college but they're not buying it. He goes to the head to take a leak and comes back to find that he's been drafted into the Marine Corps. He just about went berserk in the selective service office."

Curran looks at Davis and kind of laughs, "Next thing I know I hear some guy screaming that they're fucking with his mind. All these old ladies that work there start hiding behind their desks. I thought they were going to take him away in a strait jacket. We went thru Parris Island together but he really had a hard time. I thought they were going to kill him a few times."

Marshall and I glanced at each other, both happy to have missed the Parris Island experience. Within an hour or so the company returned under the supervision of one Sergeant E-5. They were a grubby looking lot in their unstarched, wrinkled utilities and covers. Little did I realize then that soon Marshall and I would look like that as well. After the troops were dismissed, we approached the E-5 and Marshall reported in,

"Sergeant, Lance Corporal Marshall and PFC Daley reporting as ordered."

His name tag said "Johnson" and he looked puzzled as he stared at the two of us in our starched utilities and shiny boots, "What do you guys want?"

I responded, "We're here to go thru ITR, Sergeant."

I could tell that Johnson was still not quite getting it, "You guys are here to go thru ITR? Are you shitting me or what?"

The basic problem was that after two or three months in the Marine Corps and another few months in Casual Company, we probably were "saltier" and looked more squared away than he did. He was definitely having a hard time getting his head around the idea. Marshall came right to the point, "That's the deal. We dropped from OCS and we're here for ITR."

Johnson had probably already had a tough day and by now he just wanted to get us out of his face, "Okay! Okay! Daley, you're in 1st platoon. Marshall, you're in 3rd platoon. Hurry up and stow your gear. You guys have to draw some equipment. We'll be heading back out to the field in about an hour."

You really had to laugh about it. Here we were trying to talk the personnel office out of sending us thru ITR and then the NCO at ITR can't believe we're supposed to go thru it. Before too long, however, I wouldn't be laughing.

CHAPTER ELEVEN

ITR

ITR would prove to be a different experience for Marshall and myself. It would involve a lot less in the way of personal harassment and much more in the way of pure weapons training. This approach, of course, was posited on the assumption that everyone was in good physical shape based on their training at Parris Island or, in our case, Quantico, and it was now time to teach us how to use all the weapons available to a Marine Corps infantryman. The weather at Geiger would also prove to be a significant factor for everyone, but, particularly for Marshall and myself. The two of us had gone thru Quantico in the dead of winter and it was an entirely different cat than North Carolina in the middle of summer. At Quantico, it had been seventeen degrees with snow and ice, the extra weight of field jackets, and your hands so sore most of the time that you couldn't bend them. Now we would be out in the field where the temperature hovered between ninety and one hundred degrees with humidity approaching one hundred percent, most of the time. We would be working our way thru various firing ranges and crawling around in the heat and that sandy, dusty soil on one canteen of water a day. In retrospect, having trained in both winter and summer, it's hard to say which is worse but each, in its own way, is pretty bad. Over the next twenty days of training I would manage to lose twenty pounds, about a pound per day, due to a lack of and the poor quality of the food as well as the heat and humidity of the local climate.

My introduction to 1st Platoon was not without incident either. I had barely walked thru the doors of the squad bay when a commotion started. Double-decker bunks were flying and a wall locker went over as two enlisted men started "slugging it out." One of them, I would learn in the next few minutes, had been the acting platoon sergeant up until now. It appeared that one of his charges had taken issue with something he had said or done and the first stages of a full mutiny were now underway. Right behind me through the door was Johnson, moving on the double, "Okay! Okay you two! Break it up. What the shit is going on?"

Amidst the babble of responding voices he suddenly held up his hands, "Okay! Forget it! I don't want to hear it. Where the hell are those two guys from OCS?"

Much as it pained me to do so, I stepped forward and raised my hand, "Here, Sergeant. I'm Daley. Marshall is in 3rd Platoon."

Johnson looked in my direction, "Daley, as of now, you're the platoon sergeant for 1st Platoon and I don't want to hear any more shit from anyone. Got it?"

I nodded my head resignedly, "I got it."

Johnson turned on his heel to leave, stopped suddenly, turned again and said, "And tell Marshall that he's the Acting Company Gunny as of right now."

As Johnson departed I turned to see all eyes in the squad bay on me. Wondering what my next move should be I asked, "Who's the platoon guide?"

A tall black guy who looked powerfully built stepped forward, "That'd be me. I'm Rush."

At that moment I thanked the Lord for giving me such a powerful looking assistant. I also reminded myself to never get on the wrong side of him, "Rush, I'm Daley. You know all these guys and I don't so I'm going to need your help keeping things squared away."

I saw a hint of a smile on his face and I knew I had made some points with Rush, if not with the whole platoon. Rush looked like a powerful ally and I congratulated myself on this brilliant stroke of statesmanship. Rush might have been next in line to be platoon sergeant. This way he was still pretty much in charge and the platoon apparently knew and respected him. Better yet, they might fear him. For all of the above reasons, my life would be easier. Rush nodded, "Not a problem. I got it covered."

Immediately after that we heard Johnson bellow, "M Company, get outside. Fall in. Move it."

And with those fateful words, I knew that Marshall and I were back "in the shit." We were once again carrying a rifle, a light marching pack, and a full belt that included two magazines, a canteen, and a first aid kit. For some reason, no bayonets were issued. I wondered if that were a precautionary move adhered to when training "snuffies." Johnson briefed us quickly relative to the fact that we would start off our training with a few simple exercises and then things would intensify over the next three weeks or so. He did have one more interesting note to add, "There are lots of snakes out here. We need them for training so don't kill them unless they bite you. If a snake bites you we'll need to know if it's poisonous or not and how to treat you. If they don't bite you leave them alone."

I saw a few eyes widen as this news registered and I thought I saw Johnson snicker as he turned to lead us out.

Our first day out was relatively easy. It was really hot and humid and we were all sweating pretty good but the marching pace wasn't too bad. It did get a little hairy when they had us practicing the "low crawl" with our noses down in that sandy soil. It was so damn hot and dusty that I felt like I couldn't catch my breath but that was the worst of it. From then on it was a question of marching out to the field in the morning, going thru a number of different firing ranges or individual movement courses and marching back in the evening. While we were in the field we usually ate "C" rations which weren't all that bad, given the quality of the food at the mess hall. I could eat almost anything out of a can with the exception of ham and lima beans. Those I really hated and I always traded them off for almost anything else. Even ham and eggs in a "C" ration can wasn't too bad. You would open the can, light up your little sterno can to heat the stuff up, and chow down.

One of the first weapons courses was the grenade range. The range consisted of a series of round bunkers with walls about three feet high constructed of sandbags. There was also a tower where the fire control instructor stood. Each marine would enter the bunker and lay face down with your hands clasped behind your neck until the individual instructor in each bunker nudged the prone trainee in the side with his boot tip and said something endearing like, "Get up dummy."

You would then stand up and extend your arm out with your palm up and respond, "Ready, sir."

The fire control instructor would then say, "Take grenade."

The instructor would place the grenade in your hand and you would immediately pull the grenade in to your chest and hold it there. The fire control instructor would then say, "Prepare to pull pin."

Each marine would grasp the pin. The next order would be, "Pull pin."

You were then holding a live grenade minus the pin to your chest but with the spoon still held down. If you "milked the grenade" by moving your fingers around on the spoon or dropped it in the bunker you and your instructor were more or less history. There were a number of stories about trainees who had dropped a grenade in the bunker. This "action" was usually followed by the "reaction" of both the instructor and the trainee diving head first over the outside walls of the bunker. The next command was, "Prepare to throw."

You extended your arm still holding the grenade and then came the final command, "Throw."

You then threw the grenade as far as possible and hit the dirt facedown as quickly as possible with both hands over the back of your neck.

One of the grenade range instructors was a black gunnery sergeant, seemingly, just hanging back and observing. If you screwed up, however, you quickly learned his function. He would holler, "Come over here dummy."

You then became acquainted with his weapon of choice, a ball peen hammer which he would quickly bring down on the top of your helmet about a half dozen times. It was a bit like being in the bell tower of a church while the bell is ringing. In a way, it was kind of funny to watch, unless you happened to be the transgressor. To a certain extent, you also had to admire the ingenuity of the various instructors as they vied to get your undivided attention.

We then moved on to the range for the 3.5 rocket launcher, better known in some circles as the "bazooka." This range consisted of a half dozen bunkers from which we fired. The control tower was positioned behind us. In the open field in front of us were the rusting hulks of a half dozen tanks. Marshall and I had paired off for this firing exercise. One of us would load while the other fired and then we would switch off. Like the grenade range, this one was fairly dangerous for a number of reasons. Being out of position either in front of or behind the rocket launcher could easily prove fatal. The rocket itself would easily take your head off and the exhaust from the rocket would blow you away as well. The firing exercise was strictly under control of the firing tower. With a bunch of rookies on the line the troop handlers were understandably nervous and in no mood for mistakes of omission or commission.

To start the exercise you checked to make sure the safety was on and you then placed the rocket launcher on your shoulder keeping weapon pointed downrange at all times. You placed your hand on your helmet and sounded off, "Hands off, safety on."

The command from the tower then came, "Load."

Your designated partner in crime would slip the rocket into the back of the tube and tap you on the helmet to indicate the weapon was now loaded. The range instructor would then continue, "Range 350."

You placed the 350 line of the circular sight right under the target and the instructor continued, "Safety off. Prepare to fire. Fire."

After firing, you then put the weapon back on safety, placed your hand on your helmet and sounded off again, "Hands off, safety on."

If you deviated in any way from the prescribed sequence you were in "deep shit."

Marshall and I both bounced our first shot in on our designated tank based on the ranging provided. You would then either increase or decrease the range based on the spotter's instructions and the sight on the weapon, "Up fifty. Down twenty-five."

It was at this point in the firing exercise that Private Davis, in another firing position on the firing line began to show serious signs of "losing it." He apparently had weathered being drafted into the Marine Corps and, somehow, he had survived Parris Island but the strain of his experiences to date appeared to be taking its toll. During the course of his relay on the firing line he appeared to be totally confused as to what he was to do. This was not lost on the first lieutenant who was running the control tower, "Get that guy off the firing line. He's crazy."

As the lieutenant stood on the tower ranting and raving at him, Davis turned around towards the tower, weapon still in hand and said, "Excuse me sir?"

That lieutenant was rendered speechless, lost all color from his face, and almost fell backward off the tower as he looked down the barrel of that 3.5 rocket launcher. A troop handler nearby leaped to his rescue, grasping the weapon by the barrel and forcing the firing end down range again while grasping Davis by the collar and throwing him backward off the firing line. Had the launcher gone off while pointed at the tower, both the tower and the first lieutenant standing on it would have been a memory, at best. As far as I could tell, that lieutenant had come mighty close to "buying the farm." Davis worried me as well. He could easily make a mistake on another range and blow any one of us away.

One of the most frightening ranges, at least to me, was the flame thrower. It actually consisted of an open field about half the length of a football field and almost as wide. Along one side were wooden bleachers. The company marched in, was dismissed and took seats in the bleachers. Two enlisted men were in the middle of the field, each with the flame thrower tanks strapped to his back. In their hands the enlisted men held the tubular snout of the flame thrower. Another enlisted man assisted in turning some valves on the tanks and igniting the end of the tube. One enlisted man aimed and a stream of fire leapt out at least one hundred fifty feet before he shut it down. This was definitely a scary weapon. I could hear murmuring in the bleachers as the troops pictured themselves with this potential inferno strapped to their backs. None of us was looking forward to this firing exercise.

Fortunately, fate in the form of a leaky tank intervened to save us. The tank on one of the flame throwers was apparently leaking and you could clearly see the shirt on one of the enlisted man demonstrating the unit, darken with whatever was leaking. Given the volatile nature of the weapon, this did not look good. Johnson huddled with the range supervisor before announcing that, due to faulty equipment, the company would not be firing the flamethrower. You could almost hear a collective sigh of relief go up from the troops.

Only slightly less frightening than the flamethrower experience was the opportunity for each of us to blow a half pound of TNT, preferably, without blowing ourselves up with it. The blast area was what appeared to be a large pit surrounded by high walls of sand. The flattened base of the pit was appeared to be about fifty feet by fifty feet, and this area was about fifteen to twenty feet deeper than the surrounding terrain. We would blow the charges by squad. Each squad contains thirteen men. If you know anything about explosives, you know that TNT itself is not necessarily volatile but a blasting cap inserted in the center of the block of TNT and ignited by a fuse has the desired effect. Each member of the squad was instructed to select a rectangular chunk of TNT with a small hole in the center as well as a fuse with a manual igniter on the end of it. The range master then approached each squad member, instructed them to hold the fuse above their helmet and crimped the blasting cap on the end of the fuse. Your hand was kept above your head so that, in the event that the highly volatile blasting cap exploded, you would lose only your hand and not your head. The cap with the fuse attached was inserted into the block of TNT. We then marched into the blasting pit as a squad, placed the charges on the ground, began to ignite the fuses, one by one, in squad order, and then walked out of the pit. I have to tell you that the thirteenth man was really starting to sweat as he watched the other twelve fuses burn and waited for his opportunity to ignite his fuse and vacant the premises. When those thirteen pieces of TNT did ignite, it was definitely a serious explosion.

Our "squad" was a relatively small one consisting of Marshall, myself, two other platoon sergeants, Rush and two other platoon guides. We went last, and, having seen all the other squads go through it, we were pretty calm about the process. If the fuses were long enough to not blow up the thirteenth man in a squad, the seventh man in our squad had no concerns. As we emerged from the pit, Johnson instructed one of the relatively nervous kids in one of the platoons to pick up the remaining open box of TNT charges. He did not look happy about the assignment. As he quickly passed our group in more than a little hurry to be rid of the box of explosive materials, Johnson lit up a fuse and threw it in the box. Chuckling at the panicked look that appeared on the enlisted man's face he said, "Here, take this with you."

Now the private was really "hot footing" it towards the rear of the company in order to get rid of the now smoking box of TNT, "This isn't funny. This thing is lit."

Marshall, myself, and most of the company couldn't help but laugh at his discomfort. Had that smoking fuse had a blasting cap crimped on it, we most definitely would not have been laughing and most likely would have been "making tracks" out of the general area.

Although I had seen the use of tear gas in many gangster movies, I had never truly experienced its effects until ITR. We all drew gas masks and Johnson went to great pains to explain how to put the mask on, clear it and seal it. As he closed out his lecture, we were all standing in a relatively large clearing in the woods and he asked, "Are there any questions? Do you guys know how to do this?"

Hearing no questions, Johnson casually turned his back pulled the pins on two gas canisters and tossed them into the middle of the group. Another E-5 tossed two more gas canisters and suddenly the three platoons were engulfed in tear gas. I'm not sure what Johnson actually expected to happen but it sure didn't develop as planned. A few of us struggled to get our masks on and clear them but most of the group simply started hollering and heading for the woods. Unable to clear my mask and getting plenty of gas inside it, I decided to hit the dirt, reasoning that the gas would rise. Surprisingly, Johnson didn't seem too perturbed by this turn of events. In retrospect, I suppose it was because he knew what was coming later in the form of the gas chamber.

The gas chamber was a sort of shack that could accommodate perhaps six to eight men at a time. It had a unit in the center that continuously generated tear gas. You put your gas mask on, sealed it, and entered the chamber. Each man had a number and when your number was called, you removed your mask and stated your name, rank and serial number. Very shortly thereafter, you could not help but take a breath and when you did you felt as if your stomach was coming up into your throat. It was a bit like having the "dry heaves." When they felt that you had been sufficiently inundated with tear gas, they opened the door on the other side of the chamber and you were ordered to run in order to refill your lungs with air. It was a most unpleasant experience and now I knew why Johnson had not been more upset about the troops heading for the hills when the canisters had been dropped earlier. He knew what was coming in the chamber and that there would no escaping that experience.

As we entered the first week of July, we encountered the Individual Movement Course. The course was a depressing, scarred piece of landscape. As you looked at it from the side there were half a dozen old water-cooled machine guns to your left on what appeared to be on fixed mounts. To our right were a series of man-made sandy hills. The course itself included strands of wire, concertina wire, wooden obstacles and what appeared to be shell holes. The course itself was perhaps seventy or eighty yards in length and about forty yards wide. At the base of the sandy hills were six trenches about a foot deep, two feet wide and twelve to fourteen feet long. The trenches almost looked like overly long graves. We would go thru the course by squad with two men in each trench, initially lying on their backs with their rifle positioned lengthwise on their chest. Each of the two men in a trench was designated either "First Relay" or "Second Relay." When your relay was called you had to emerge from the trench and crawl the length of the course "under fire." My initial thought was that the machine guns were for show only and that they were probably loaded with blanks. As we lay in our trenches looking up I heard the command, "Machine gunners test your weapons."

Suddenly I saw tracers screaming overhead and sand kicked up from the small sandy hills behind us as the bullets struck. I knew then that it wasn't all for show. Those were real bullets, and, although the rounds were fired three to four feet over our heads from machine guns that were on fixed mounts, it was still frightening to see live rounds that close. There were two standing orders, "Do not stand up under any circumstances or those machine guns will cut you in half. Do not crawl into any of the shell holes. There are live charges in them that will be ignited during the exercise."

I was the second relay in our group when the command came, "First relay on line."

Unfortunately, the kid who had been paired with me would not come out of the trench. Whether he was paralyzed with fear or not, I don't know but he wouldn't come out. The troop handlers were beside themselves, "Get out of that hole you son of a bitch. You better move."

But he stayed put.

I was desperate to do the exercise and be done with it. Finally, I clambered out of the trench and started crawling towards the end. I figured that the sooner I went, the sooner I'd be done with it. I didn't think about it I just kept crawling. I never looked back for the other kid. I just kept "motoring." In the process, I tore up my elbows by trying to crawl using my elbows to dig in and move myself forward. When our group finished the range master went nuts, "You guys are the slowest group to ever traverse this course. I ought to make you do it again. Get out of my sight. You make me sick."

We were all unimpressed by his screaming. We just wanted to get the hell out of there. I wandered down the side of the course and watched Marshall's group go through. Dave crawled up next to one of the shell holes just as they ignited a charge. I saw Marshall lifted right off the ground by the blast. His ears would be ringing tonight.

On the Fourth of July, we had an off day. After all, it was a national holiday. We now had six training days remaining in ITR. I spent Independence Day at Sick Bay happily getting all the blisters on my feet lanced and my elbows wrapped in ace bandages to protect the damage done on the Individual Movement Course.

CHAPTER TWELVE

THE QUALITY OF MERCY

There are individuals who clearly don't belong in the Marine Corps. I happily count myself among them and I'm sure that Marshall, Hinkle, Dank, Vredeveld, Lamb and Cullen all felt about the same. But with all of us, it was a little different. We were able to do it. We could "hack it" as the Marine Corps loves to say but we didn't like it. We didn't want to do it. We just didn't want to be an active member of what appeared to be this "mindless mass of green." Elite fighters though they might be, that total focus, that absence of any form of flexibility was anathema to all of us who thought that we had a brain and might do better if allowed to control our own fate. But, our "lack of belonging", if you want to call it that was essentially one of choice, perhaps precipitated by injury and a period of intense reflection in Casual Company.

There were others that we encountered in ITR, however, that fell into quite a different category. They truly did not "belong" from the "get go." I remember one individual in our Company in ITR who never carried a rifle. A Marine in formation not carrying a rifle when everyone else is, is something that you tend to notice He was a tall, well-built kid and, every time we formed up, he was carrying a stretcher instead of a rifle. I asked Curran what the story was. Curran looked at the kid with obvious admiration and said, "That guy has got more guts than anybody I know. We went thru Parris Island with him. He belongs to some religious group that doesn't believe in violence but his draft board refused to give him conscientious objector status. Then, they drafted him into the Marine Corps. Every time they handed him a rifle at Parris Island, he would lay it on the ground. Those drill instructors went berserk. They beat the shit out of him but he refused to carry that rifle. Eventually, they graduated him and I understand that they're in the process of transferring him to the Navy as a corpsman."

It really was an amazing story. Based on my own experience with drill instructors and troop handlers, I couldn't picture anyone with enough guts to refuse to carry a rifle. I know that I didn't have that kind of commitment or guts. And then one morning, as it often happened in the Marine Corps, he was gone. He just wasn't there anymore. No one explained. No one said that he had been transferred. Maybe they even gave him a general discharge but I doubted it. I'd seen people with their bodies mangled by both training and enemy fire still in the Marine Corps. Once they had you by the throat, particularly in the middle of the Viet Nam War, there was no way they were going to let you go. He was simply gone, never to be spoken of again. It reminded me of those days in OCS at Quantico when guys with pneumonia would be carried out of the squad bay in the middle of the night. But, this guy was not someone easily forgotten.

And then there was the kid in our platoon that kept disappearing every time we went out in the field. Before we would return to the squad bay at the end of the day, we were always obligated to take a count to make sure that we didn't leave anyone out in the "boonies", either injured or just lost.

Every time that Rush and I took the count we had everyone but when we got back and took another count, we were always light one man. Because our platoon was the one missing a man, we were obligated to go back out in the field and look for him. Of course, we never found him. The "M.P.'s" usually picked him up either on his way to or at New Bern Airport. This kid really wanted out of the Marine Corps in a big way and he kept going over the hill. The third time this happened, both the platoon and I were ready to kill him. Nothing is worse than having to go back out after a long hot day in the field. All you want to do is hit the showers and collapse. My protests to Johnson, however, were in vain, "Sergeant, this kid is not laying out in the field somewhere. He's halfway to the airport."

But Johnson was not to be moved. He was going by the book and rightly so, "He might be injured and laying out in the woods somewhere. Take your platoon and get out there and look for him."

As we marched back out in the field, my comment to Rush on the subject was short and sweet, "If I find that son of a bitch out there, I'm going to bury him there."

Finally, the Marine Corps decided that they had seen enough and he was gone as well. No one said he's doing brig time or he got ninety days for unlawful absence. He just simply disappeared. No one in our platoon was sorry to see him go and we didn't even discuss it. We just knew that we wouldn't have to go back out in the field at the end of a long training day to look for this "turkey." That was good enough for us.

The one that always weighed on my mind, though, was Davis. If you couldn't feel for him, you really had no heart at all. The truth was he probably should never have been drafted at all. He was married and going to school. Unfortunately, his wife was not pregnant and he was only taking nine credits instead of the required twelve. Worst of all, not only did they draft him but they drafted him into the Marine Corps. Somehow, he had managed to survive Parris Island but I could almost see him coming apart at the seams beginning with my first day at ITR. Then there was the incident with the rocket launcher. Looking back on it now, he must have already been "going around the bend" by then. The turning point was probably when they didn't pay him.

We had been in training ten days, maybe two weeks, when we received our first pay check. In those days, the pay for a private or a PFC was really "peanuts" but it was something. I guess it was almost a "confirmation" of your existence as a person. The Marine Corps had us for at least two years and they could "shit on us" virtually every day of the week but they still had to pay us. As with most things in the Marine Corps, we had to line up to get paid. I remember standing in a line with a guy for something one time and he turned to me and said, "When I get out of the Marine Corps, I'm never going to stand in a line again in my life."

Sometimes when I'm standing in line at the bank or the super market, I think of that.

When Davis reached the front of the line and gave them his name and serial number they said they didn't have his name on the roster. I'm sure he thought they were "pulling his chain" as we all did. Marshall and I didn't really expect to get paid because of our transfer from Quantico but, surprisingly, they had us on the roster. But they didn't have Davis. When Davis finally realized that they weren't kidding and they didn't have his name or his pay, he kind of hesitated at the head of the line then turned to the side looking a little dazed. Surely, this was the ultimate insult. To have gone thru all of this and now he was not even going to get paid. And, of course, as it is always done in the Marine Corps, we all piled it on a bit more, "Hey, Davis, it's probably all a mistake. You're not really in the Marine Corps after all."

Davis laughed as well but somehow this last thing had really taken it out of him. He looked like a man who has just been kicked in the stomach.

Towards the end of our training, the troop handlers would tend to look the other way when some of the troops would sneak down to the "Slop Chute" for a cold beer after coming back in from the field. Davis was one of the guys who was sucking up a few beers one night when his brother-in-law arrived at company headquarters, unexpectedly, hoping to see him for a few minutes. Unable to locate Davis, his brother-in-law finally left. When Davis returned to the company area, they told him that they had been looking for him because he had a visitor but couldn't find him. I guess it was all just too much for him, especially after a few beers. He accused the troop handler of deliberately preventing him from seeing his brother-in-law. As the story goes, Johnson, being a decent guy was willing to let it slide but then the unthinkable happened. Davis totally lost it and jumped Johnson. At that point, it was pretty much out of Johnson's hands. The story spread quickly and the word was that Davis was being held at Company Headquarters. By morning, he was gone as well but this one was different. It was almost as if none of us could look each other in the eye. We wondered to ourselves if we could have done more to help him. Perhaps our "ragging him" about not getting paid and not actually being in the Marine Corps had been the "final straw." We had to assume that he drew some brig time for jumping Johnson and none of us could picture Davis surviving that. Maybe, they discharged him as "Section 8" or with some sort of general discharge.

Over the years, I've thought about Davis a lot. In those days we were all up to our eye balls with the Marine Corps' bullshit and we had little time or concern for anyone else. All we wanted to do was go home. Davis shouldn't have been there to start with but none of us seemed willing to help him survive something for which he was not equipped. The "stretcher bearer" was certainly tough enough to make it on his own and the kid who kept going "over the hill" was probably beyond help. But, Davis, that was another story. Sometimes I still see his face, sweating, eyes shifting back and forth nervously, a confused half smile on his face as he tries to decide whether to laugh or cry, and I wonder what became of him.

Certainly Shakespeare said it best, "The quality of mercy is not strained...."

Unfortunately, none of us chose to "strain the quality of mercy" for Davis.

CHAPTER THIRTEEN

THE GREAT ESCAPE

We were now closing in on the end of our training in ITR. There were only a few days remaining when the weather suddenly changed. We marched out to the field early one morning in a driving rain, wearing basically the same gear except now we also wore ponchos in a futile attempt to stay dry. Our first stop would be the M-60 machine gun range where we would learn to both disassemble and reassemble the machine gun and fire it as well. After that we would practice some tactics in the field using blanks and then, finally, we would walk the "John Wayne Course" using live ammunition. "John Wayne" involved walking down a path with your rifle at "high port" and pointed downrange, firing a prescribed number of rounds at each man-sized target that you encountered, reloading once and then firing at the remaining targets as you traversed the balance of the course. "John Wayne" made me very nervous. As a platoon sergeant I would be leading a squad and I worried about some huckleberry behind me with a full clip not keeping his weapon pointed downrange. It was one of those ranges where it would very easy to get killed. I'd seen a few of these turkeys in action already and it had not bolstered my confidence or my morale.

The night before we had been out in the field late doing a night compass march and searching for trip wires on a darkened path. It had been close to midnight by the time we had gotten back in. The lack of sleep and the weather had only served to make us all more irritable, hopefully, not more careless. A kid from the Bronx named Daniels had been my point man for the night compass march. You essentially figured out the desired heading by clicks on the compass, each click representing so many degrees of compass. You then send a man out far enough that you can see him, point the compass at him, and advance the squad. Then you repeat the exercise. Daniels had had a tough night. Being a city boy he was not thrilled with woods at night. Even as I was sending him out as point man he kept protesting, "Come on, man. That's far enough. That's it."

The fact that he had fallen down a hill backwards while I was sending him out had not helped matters. One minute he was there to sight on and the next minute he was gone accompanied by some appropriate words of wisdom, "Shit, man. That's it. I almost got killed out there."

At this point, of course, the squad was in stitches. A little later that evening, the squad had advanced down a path on hands and knees looking for trip wires. Each man held onto the belt of the man in front of him. If you hit a trip wire, all kinds of flares went off and your squad was essentially dead. To our right and left were other squads doing the same thing. Suddenly, there was a huge uproar about two lanes to our right. People were whooping and hollering and flares were going off. We could hear someone shouting, "Shit! There's a snake over here. Damn, I just about grabbed him by the tail."

I froze for the moment but then started down the path again, my squad pretty much in linked step. Just then I heard a slight rustle to my right and what sounded like a hissing sound. I froze once again. Daniels, still holding on to my belt, was the first to respond, "What's going on?"

I remained still and listened but could hear nothing, "I don't know. I thought I heard something that sounded like a snake."

Now, I had Daniels' full attention, "A snake? Shit, man, let's get out of here."

Suddenly, our whole squad was going backwards down the infiltration path, still holding on to each other's belts. What a sight we must be I thought to myself. How about, "Backpedal, march."

Shortly thereafter, Johnson hollered, "All right, you turkeys, stand up. As far as I'm concerned, none of you completed the course. I am not impressed. Turn around and get back into formation."

We had then marched back into the squad bays. Although he was growling a bit, my sense was that Johnson was not all that concerned about tonight's outcome. He was probably as tired as we were of crawling around in the boonies. Our training was almost done and he was probably as anxious to end it as we were.

As we approached the M-60 range the following morning, the rain was still coming down in sheets. There were three M-60 machine guns set up, presumably for instruction. The M-60 was a brutal looking weapon with a wooden stock, suitable for walking assaults and a tripod to steady it when firing from a fixed emplacement. It had a tremendous rate of fire and was belt fed. For those familiar with the movie "First Blood", the M-60 is Rambo's weapon of choice in the final scenes of the movie. Each platoon huddled around a weapon as the instructor quickly disassembled and then reassembled it. Four men from each platoon held a tent half over each instructor and weapon to shield them from the rain as he worked. We, on the other hand, stood in the rain and watched. When the instructor had gone through it once we were told to pair off and one man would disassemble the weapon while the other would reassemble it. As each pair finished working with the weapon, they were shifted to the firing range.

I paired off with Marshall and, fortunately, he had been watching the instructor while I had been silently cursing our fate as we stood in the teeming rain in the middle of the woods. Marshall quickly broke the weapon down and with his help I managed to get it back together. At least, there were no pieces left over. Of course, we did not get the benefit of a tent half. We had to work with the rain streaming down our helmets and either off our ponchos or down our necks. That was one of the moments when I really hated the Marine Corps. We then shifted to the firing range where Marshall and I again paired off together to fire the weapon. One man loaded the belt and closed the breech. The second man cocked the weapon and then fired on the instructor's order. There were half a dozen M-60's set up to fire at a bunker constructed out of logs which was about fifty to seventy five yards away. The instructor looked at Marshall and me and said, "Lay down."

I looked down at the four inch deep puddle at my feet as if to say "Where" but I thought better of it. I lay down in the four inches of muddy water and felt it soak through my utilities under my poncho and thought to myself, "Time flies when you're having fun."

I loaded the belt and Marshall cocked the weapon. On the instructor's command six M-60's proceeded to obliterate the bunker. I watched in amazement as big chunks of wood went flying as the rounds hit the logs, imagining what those rounds might do to a human body. We then switched positions. Marshall loaded and, on the command, I pulled the trigger. Unfortunately, I had forgotten to cock the weapon and the instructor was not amused. I could see him heading our way in a hurry, "Shit!"

I quickly cocked the weapon and, trying not to smoke the barrel, fired off thirty-five rounds in a series of bursts of five to seven rounds. The instructor was pissed that I had forgotten to cock the weapon but pleased that I had recovered so quickly and remembered not to burn out the barrel while managing to tear up the target with well-directed rounds. By the time he had taken two steps in our direction, it was all over and he had decided to ignore the transgression. Marshall looked at me quizzically as if he knew my mind was somewhere else, anywhere else, "Well, no shit, Daley! Are you on vacation or something?"

I just grimaced and he got the message without the benefit of a meaningful answer, "Something like that."

By the time we got around to eating something, it was still raining. It was "C" rations once again. We looked like a bunch of hobos as we hunkered down in our ponchos around our little sterno cans, heating up our "C" rations. As I glanced around at this scene, soaking wet with sand working its way around under my poncho, I thought to myself, "This must be how it looked during the Great Depression. Tell me again why I'm doing this."

After chow we did some more "snooping and pooping" in the boonies, using blanks and practicing squad maneuvers, advancing fire teams with covering fire, and finally doing a walking assault on a fixed position. Finally, it stopped raining and we could chuck the ponchos, clean as much sand as possible off of our gear, particularly our M-14's, and we got ready for "John Wayne." Marshall and I helped hand out the live ammo, saying our prayers all the while. Each man received forty rounds or two full clips. Once the clips were loaded, we broke down into squads and waited to start the course.

It wasn't all that long before a problem occurred. Someone in the squad ahead of us was apparently waving his weapon around a little carelessly and Johnson reacted immediately. He grabbed the rifle with his left hand, keeping it down range, grabbed the marine by the back of his collar and flung him backwards off the line while still grasping the M-14. In one fluid motion, he crouched down and emptied the twenty-round clip down range, "You dumb shit! Are you trying to kill someone or what? Get the hell out of my sight."

That incident gave me a panicky feeling in my gut and an itching between my shoulder blades as I thought of the twelve "snuffies" behind me in line. Each one was carrying two full clips and none, with the exception of Rush, inspired any confidence in me.

Soon, it was our turn to push off. The rules of the game were pretty straight forward. You fired two rounds at the first target, three at the second and so on, emptying your clip at the last target before the reload point. You didn't use the sights on the rifle but rather fired three to four inches over the sights, snapping in on a target that was ten to fifteen yards away to your left as the squad moved from left to right. You kept your finger outside the trigger guard and the safety was on until you turned to fire. The safety itself was inside the trigger guard, just in front of the trigger, and you pushed it forward to release it. You were supposed to use your thumb to release the safety but I found that awkward and tended to use my index finger. The targets were man-sized figures behind small piles of sand, such that the upper body was visible. Some targets popped up and some were stationary. Just before the reload point, I flicked the safety off and fired my last three rounds at the target with a troop handler in front of and to the right of me. He started to jump in my shit about releasing the safety with my index finger, "Which finger did you use to release that safety?"

I started to answer, "I used my index finger because it's too hard to get your thumb in there..."

As he prepared to "jump in my shit", he happened to glance at the target and noted that my first shot had gone thru the top of the sand hill and drilled the target in the gut, the second hit the middle of the chest, and the third was in the forehead. The pattern of the shots appeared to ease the tension of the moment, "Nice shooting, but, I want you to use your thumb. Like this. You can do it. Get going."

At the reload point, I released the clip in the weapon and snapped in the second clip, pulling it slightly forward and then snapping it back with the rifle butt on the ground and the muzzle at a forty-five degree angle down range, as always. The rest of the course was routine and I even lived to tell about it which made it a good day.

As we finished up the course there was a commotion further down along the tree line and the sound of about ten or fifteen shots. Marshall and I both looked around, "What the hell was that?"

One of the guys passing us on the way back said that a bunch of those "huckleberries" from the hills had seen a rabbit and the troop handlers had let them open up on it with some live rounds that were left over, "Man, they just shot the shit out of that thing."

I looked at Marshall, "Terrific. I needed to hear that. Let's get the fuck out of here."

And as quickly as it had all begun, it ended. We were back at the squad bay, turning in field gear, cleaning up, and packing our sea bags as the orders started to come down. A bunch of guys were drawing orders for AIT or Advanced Infantry Training. That meant that their MOS would be "0300." They were going to be infantry or as they say in the Corps "grunts." I thought to myself, "Lucky them! Viet Nam was definitely in their future, albeit a short future."

Other guys were drawing orders to specific schools, depending upon their MOS. That meant that they could stay out of "the shit" for a least a few more months before getting shipped to

"Staging" at Camp Pendleton for further training. "Staging" would be followed closely by orders to "WestPac" or Western Pacific.

As far as Marshall and I were concerned, nothing was happening. We received no orders and when we asked about it we were told, "They might be at Battalion Headquarters but we don't have anything yet so sit tight."

One day went by and then another and still there were no orders. At this point, it was Marshall and I and no one else remaining in the company. Hinkle dropped in and it turned out that his company had deployed and he was still waiting as well. This didn't look good and we all began to speculate on what kind of special horror the Marine Corps had in mind for three "OC drops." Hinkle's anxiety level was on the rise now. "Shit, man. I bet we're getting shipped to Viet Nam. They didn't send us to Parris Island but they're going to make up for it now."

Marshall was still maintaining his cool, "I'm not buying it. They don't give a shit about us one way or the other. Something else is going on. Maybe they're sitting on our orders while they decide what to do with us."

Hinkle mentioned that he had seen Dank, Vredeveld, and Lamb in another company but they were still in training so you couldn't tell anything from what they were doing, "I still think they're fucking with us and that is definitely not good. I don't know what they have in mind but, knowing the Marine Corps, I'm pretty sure that we're not going to like it. Shit! I should have stayed at Quantico."

I was worried too but Hinkle's bitching was giving me a headache, "Yeah, right. If you had stayed at Quantico you would definitely be on your way to Nam in the not too distant future. I agree with Dave. Somebody's trying to figure out what to do with us. We need to find out where our orders are and what's going on."

It was Marshall who hit on it, "Listen, I'm thinking that there have to be some of our guys in Battalion Headquarters. I mean "OC drops." It just goes to figure. I say we go up there and nose around. We'll tell them we're worried about our orders and see what they can tell us. The "lifers" won't tell us shit but the "OC drops", if there are any, might. What do you say?"

And so it was agreed that we would wait until later that afternoon to hit on Battalion Headquarters and check out Marshall's theory, hoping that the "lifers" had checked out early. We had figured it pretty well. When we hit Battalion Headquarters the place was empty except for a corporal and a lance corporal. Marshall gave them his pitch, "We're Marshall and Daley from "M" Company and this is Hinkle from "O" Company and we're trying to track down our orders. We finished training a couple of days ago but nothing has come down for us. We thought maybe you guys could tell us something."

The two kind of glanced at each other and the lance corporal said, "We did see orders for you guys. I think they're on the First Sergeant's desk. They need to be signed."

Marshall gave them his best Texas hustler's smile and said, "Okay but what's holding them up? We've been sitting down there for two days. Is there a problem with the orders?"

Now the corporal spoke, "As far as I know there's no problem. We're just waiting for a signature to send them out."

Again, he and the lance corporal glanced at each other and I could tell that Marshall had caught it too. We both knew that something was going on we just didn't know what. Marshall tried once again, "Are you guys "OC drops" as well?"

The corporal spoke now, "You got it. I'm getting out in about two weeks. I'm so short you can barely see me."

He nodded in the lance corporal's direction, "He's got about two months to go."

Marshall kind of glanced in my direction, "What's the deal on replacing you guys? Have they got someone coming in?"

Now the corporal hesitated and looked down, "Not that I'm aware of."

Now it was clear what was going on. It had registered on both of us at about the same time. They were sitting on our orders, hoping Personnel at Lejeune would forget about us and then they would have their replacements. Marshall pressed on, "Do you know where our orders were to? Where were they sending us?"

The lance corporal answered now, "I think the orders were to Lejeune but I only looked at them quickly."

Marshall and I were on the same wave length now, "Seeing as how you have our orders, how about just giving them to us and letting us get going. I don't think the guys at Camp

Lejeune are going to care if they're signed or not. If so, they just send them back for signature."

Both of them hesitated now, "I don't know about that."

But Marshall and I would not be put off that easily, "How about you tell the First Sergeant that we came looking for our orders and we found them on his desk."

The corporal and lance corporal looked at each other before the corporal answered, "Sure, why not. I'll be gone before he misses you guys."

After grabbing our orders, I had to talk my way past the gate in order to get to my car which was parked across the road. The M.P. at the gate just shrugged and said, "Go ahead. If you don't come back they'll come and get you anyhow."

Within thirty minutes Marshall and I had stowed our gear in the car, picked up Hinkle at his squad bay and we were making tracks for Camp Lejeune with three sets of unsigned orders in our hot little hands.

As we walked into the Personnel office at Lejeune with our orders and SRB's in hand, a loud voice boomed out from the back of the office, "Are you guys Marshall, Daley and Hinkle?"

The source of the voice was a squarely built gunnery sergeant with a crew cut. Marshall responded, "That's us, Gunny."

The voice boomed out again, "Where the shit have you guys been? I been looking for you for three days."

Marshall just shrugged, "Hell, Gunny. We're lucky to be here. They wouldn't give us our orders. We had to go to Battalion Headquarters and hijack them. Otherwise, we'd still be there."

The Gunny shook his head, "Those lying bastards. They told me they didn't have any orders for you guys. I want the three of you to go check into Headquarters Company for tonight. Report back here at 0800. Got it?"

Marshall answered for all three of us, "We got it. Thanks, Gunny."

Chapter Fourteen

The Man from Mississippi

True to his word Gunny Tedrick was waiting for us in the Personnel Office at 0800 the next morning. Rumor had it that Tedrick was out of West Virginia by way of a football scholarship that had left him with a damaged knee. He had then joined the Marine Corps and had become what we would have considered a "lifer", with something like fifteen years in the service already. The word was that he had been a gunner on a helicopter and was shot down twice. The sudden loss of altitude had damaged his eardrums and he had eventually ended up in Personnel. Tedrick was also bit of a "Sam Huff look alike" with his blocky middle linebacker's build. He looked fit at about five ten or eleven and two hundred pounds but still not quite as large as Huff had been when he was playing for the New York Giants. When speaking in a normal tone, Tedrick had a raspy, still too loud a voice. When making it a point to be heard and heard clearly he easily raised his voice several decibels. It was in that booming voice that he greeted us that morning, "You know, you guys are causing me a lot of work. I've been on the phone all morning with that dipshit first sergeant at your old battalion headquarters. He claims he never saw your orders so I guess you guys must have typed them up on your way over here. What an asshole! Well, at least you guys ain't like those Navy doctors that they send me. Now those sons of bitches are really something. They send them somewhere for six weeks to teach them how to wear a uniform and salute. Then they show up down here with their golf clubs in a big hurry for me to check them in."

Marshall and I couldn't help but chuckle at this last little monologue. Tedrick really was "a man for all seasons." He didn't mess with the troops unless they messed with him and he wasn't afraid to call an officer an asshole if the label fit. Tedrick's voice was back to his normal a raspy growl now, "Okay, Hinkle, you found a home in ISO. That's Information Services for those of you not familiar with Marine Corps parlance. According to your SRB, you're supposed to be some kind of hotshot reporter from The Philadelphia Inquirer. Jesus H. Christ! Is that one of those rags that makes up stories about Hollywood stars? And you're from Philadelphia, the city of brotherly love of all places? It sure as hell wasn't when I was there. Get your ass over to ISO. Walk outside and follow the signs. You can't miss it. I can't wait to read the next issue of the base newspaper."

Marshall and I got a laugh out of that one as well. Hinkle hadn't even blinked at all the near insults to his home city and former employer. He was definitely more than a little relieved at the idea that he didn't have one foot on a plane to Viet Nam and the other on a banana peel. Gunny Tedrick continued with his one-man show. "Marshall and Daley, in your cases, we have some choices. Everybody in Building One wants a piece of you two. Go see Sergeant Rogers in the office of the Assistant Chief of Staff Manpower. Just follow the signs to Building One. I know two smart boys like you can find your way that far. After that, get your asses back here."

Building One was the largest building on the base and thus tough to miss. You could have stood in front of the Personnel Office and hit it with a rock. It was where the commanding general and all the top brass hung out. Marshall and I walked the fifty yards or so, entered a side door and took an immediate left into the designated office. We entered a large ante room with three desks and two people. At one desk was a woman of about twenty-five who was attractive but not really pretty. At the other was a Sergeant E-5 with a name tag that said Rogers. He was smallish in size with straight black hair and kind of a slinky look about him. My guess was that he was an "OC drop" as well. Beyond the ante room were two additional offices. The one on the left appeared to be empty while the one on the right was occupied by two individuals, one a lieutenant colonel, the other a civilian. Rogers introduced himself and indicated that the colonel wanted to see both Marshall and myself but individually. Rogers led Marshall into the office.

After all, "rank has its privileges" and Marshall was a lance corporal while I was a mere PFC. The civilian in the office excused himself and nodded to me as he exited both the office and the ante room. Rogers closed the office door as he exited and invited me to take a seat. He also introduced the young lady as Mary-Anne, Colonel Jones' secretary. Within no more than ten minutes, Marshall exited the office with a big smile on his face and said, "Well, I'm all set. You're up, Daley."

Rogers led me into the office, placed my SRB in the center of the colonel's desk and exited. I stepped forward, centered myself on the desk and reported, "Sir, PFC Daley reporting as ordered, sir."

The "light colonel" behind the desk should have been a poster boy for the Marine Corps. Although not wearing a crew cut, his hair was cut "high and tight" and his shoulders and chest bulged under the short-sleeve open collared Dacron shirt. He was probably in his late thirties but looked at least forty-five because of the leathery texture of his face. This was Lieutenant Colonel C.B. (Blake) Webster and he looked every bit the part of a field marine. In contrast, I suddenly realized that I looked like a "bag of rags." I had lost twenty pounds in training and I was still wearing utilities that were none too clean and definitely not pressed, much less starched. With the weight loss, my web belt had six to eight inches of slack at the end of the buckle rather than the regulation four inches. Webster said nothing and did not even look up for a minute or two as he studied or at least appeared to study my service record book. Finally, he looked up and spoke, "Stand at ease, Daley."

I accepted his invitation and he appeared to relax a bit, twiddling a pencil in his hand and tapping the end on his desk as he spoke, "Here's the deal. I need two men to work in this office doing administrative work. You were in OCS so I know you're smart enough. I want to know what you want to do. Are you interested?"

Having been in the Marine Corps for six months at this time, I'd come to the point of realizing that most of the time you have no choice and simply accept what is offered, "That sounds fine, sir."

But Webster was not so easily put off, "You don't have to do this, Daley. That's why I'm asking. Would you rather stay here or would you prefer to go to Viet Nam?"

I have to admit that one of the shortcomings in my character has always been just doing the smart thing. The smart move would have been to simply say, "Thank you, sir. I'd be happy to accept an assignment here."

Although he probably never meant it that way and was probably just trying to give me a choice, somehow, I heard his words as a challenge. That is to say, take this job or I'll ship you to Viet Nam. My answer, of course, was not the "smart one", "Actually sir, either one is fine. If you want to keep me here, that's fine. If you want to ship me to Viet Nam, that's fine too. I have eighteen months to serve and then I go home."

I could tell that this was not the answer that Webster was looking for and, for a moment, just a moment, I thought I was definitely "WestPac bound." But then I saw something flicker in his eyes. Maybe it was a sense of resignation, maybe weariness, but for whatever reason, he cut me some slack, "Okay, Daley, I'm assigning you to our office. Report back here at 0800 tomorrow. How's your typing?"

Later, when I tracked down Marshall, we shared our conversations with Webster. Marshall had quickly accepted the offer and then he asked about my experience, "Well, Daley, did you jump over the desk and kiss him when he offered you a job here?"

I filled Marshall in on my session with Webster. When I was done, he just looked at me and shook his head, "You're really nuts, Daley. You just keep on playing Russian roulette. Who gives a shit what Webster or anyone else thinks now or ever? Go to Viet Nam? Not if I can help it. That'll be the fucking day. A year and a half from now I plan to be back in Dallas sucking down a cold one and the Marine Corps will be just one more bad memory."

That night, Marshall and I found a little steak house on the road into the base and we sat down to a couple of outstanding steaks with all the trimmings and more than a couple of cold ones. I had to admit, the steak house wasn't in New York but it sure did feel like heaven.

The next morning Marshall and I reported to work still dressed in utilities. Webster promptly advised us that we would have to dress in what was known as a "Class C" uniform. In the warmer months that would be khaki colored trousers and a short sleeve shirt with an open color and a khaki colored "piss cutter" for a cover. In the colder months that would be green trousers, long sleeve Dacron shirt with a tie and a green "piss cutter." No blouse was required but a field jacket could be worn in the colder months. The Marine Corps made it very easy for you. On October 15th you changed to greens and on April 15th you changed to khakis. If it was ninety degrees on October 15th, you still wore greens. If it was twenty degrees on April 15th, you still wore khakis. Absolutely no thinking on the subject of uniforms was required.

When we advised Webster that we had not drawn all our uniforms at Quantico because the expectation was that we would become officers and buy our own, he assigned Rogers to take us to Supply and get us outfitted. On the way back from supply, Rogers led us out to the parking lot to a van which we assumed was his, "I want to show you guys something. I thought you might be interested."

He reached in the back of the van and pulled out a stack of very explicit "skin magazines." We looked at him puzzled. He said, "Well, I thought you guys might want to buy these from me. I bought them in D.C. and they've given me a lot of pleasure over the last two years. I could let you have them for $20.00."

Marshall and I glanced at each other and then at the wedding band on this guy's finger, wondering, what the hell his story was. At times like those, I have to admit that I was uncomfortable being classified as an "OC drop" with guys like Rogers floating around. Maybe he just had to "shit can" the magazines before he went home so that his wife didn't see them. Dave simply said, "I don't think so. We'll keep trying to find the real thing."

I nodded my agreement.

We returned to the office and began to learn about our "partners in crime." Mary-Anne seemed like a nice lady who was simply a little "ditsy." Like most of the women working in these offices, she was married to a "lifer" who was, either, currently in Viet Nam or had just been and returned. She giggled a lot and seemed to be easily impressed by the attention paid to her by any male in the vicinity. Thinking back on her now, I remember a line that I had heard in a movie about the average southern woman in a small town, "They spend four years in high school trying to figure out who they're going to marry and the rest of their lives trying to figure out why."

Carroll Jones was the civilian that we had seen in the same office with Colonel Webster. He was a civil service employee, a GS-11 or 12, as I understood it, and some sort of manpower expert. He had been an officer in the Navy in his former life and, although a southerner from North Carolina, he seemed to have very little accent. He seemed to speak in a soft, almost mellow, monotone that could easily put you to sleep. He smoked a pipe and an occasional cigar but didn't hassle us much. Every now and then he would get a bit testy and he seemed to think that he was wearing the Colonel's oak leaves, but not very often. I took my lead from Marshall who was relatively unflappable and we tended to ignore Mr. Jones most of the time.

And now we came to know the "Man from Mississippi", Colonel States Rights Jones, Jr. Hard as it was to believe, that really was his name. Marshall summed it up real well, "His daddy didn't do him any favors. That name might play well in Mississippi or south of the Mason Dixon line, but not in a lot of other places."

He was a small man, certainly no taller than five foot six inches, with lean craggy features and closely-cropped, sandy-colored hair. His MOS was armor, that is to say, he was a tanker. Marshall and I really got a charge out of that one given what a little bitty guy he was. According to Dave, "He probably just loved driving that tank over the top of any big guys that got in his way."

Jones looked lean and fit and was almost always smoking a pipe. Occasionally you would see him light up a cigarette or a cigar, but mostly, it was a pipe. He was from a town called Benoit. Had he said that he was from Biloxi it would really have been "the limit." Jones had entered the Corps in 1942, and to hear him tell it had gone through OCS with Tyrone

Power. He would remark offhandedly, "You know, that Tyrone Power was really a nice guy and did everything that we did."

Colonel Jones had been in the Marine Corps for twenty-six years and he loved it. Somehow, Marshall had also come by the information, as only he could, that Jones had won the Silver Star in World War II. If Jones had any regrets, I would guess it was only that he had not made Brigadier General. He remained a full or "Bird Colonel." If I had any regrets, it was hearing him tell me that he also had a degree in Economics as did I. Having already relegated Jones mentally to the level of "one more red-neck from Mississippi", I now found myself having to adjust my thinking to categorize this fellow Economics major as "the enlightened man from Mississippi", if there was such a thing. Unfortunately, more for me than for Colonel Jones, I suspected that we did not like each other. We both seemed to have a healthy respect for each other but neither one of us really liked the other. Jones liked to pull my chain periodically by saying, "Too bad you never managed to pick up that commission, Daley."

I, of course, refusing to recognize the gap in rank or to cut him any slack at all, would feel obligated to reply in my usual smart-ass way, "It's not really a problem, sir. I won't be here that long. I go home in eighteen months."

We just seemed to have a talent for rubbing each other the wrong way. Later that year Colonel Jones would insist that I have Christmas dinner at his home on base. I had taken leave earlier to go home to see my brother, also on leave from the Marine Corps, and that left me stuck on base for the holidays. I kept trying to beg off but he finally made it an order that I would be there. He and his family were all very gracious and, in spite of the presence of lots of 'brass" stopping by for a drink, I was almost having a good time. It was then that Jones managed to "rain on my parade" one more time. He insisted that I have another drink. I declined but again he insisted so I gave in and he mixed me another vodka and tonic. As he returned from the kitchen after mixing the drink, he handed me the drink and said, "Drink up, Daley. That's the last time you're going to have a full Colonel serving you drinks."

The statement was almost like a slap across the face and a reminder of his perception of the difference in our stations, despite the fact that it was Christmas and I was a guest in his house. I laughed, glanced at him and said, "I guess that's true, sir. Thank you for the drink."

But somehow I knew that Jones could see the wheels turning in my head. I was actually thinking, "I don't know. You might retire and become a bartender at Schrafft's in the Chrysler building. Then you would still be serving me drinks."

And I suppose that was more or less the framework within which Colonel Jones and I would operate for the next eighteen months. He was basically a fair man and probably a "straight-shooter", but to me, he would always be symbolic of the rigidness and the inflexibility of the Marine Corps. He could be funny one minute and a real pain in the ass the next minute. Back in the days when such things were easily overlooked, he would come into the office in the morning singing a little ditty to thrill his secretary, "Oh, she jumped in bed, covered up her head and said you cannot find me. I knew damn well she lied like hell and jumped right in behind her."

His secretary would laugh nervously and say, "Oh my goodness, Colonel."

On another occasion he promoted me to sergeant and then promptly chewed me out for not standing at attention properly.

And so that was the nature of our relationship. Jones was the officer and I was the enlisted man and neither one of us was willing to cut the other much slack. As I said, we seemed to respect one another but we definitely did not like one another. And to say that we had diverse views on the Marine Corps would have been the understatement of the century. Marshall, on the other hand, seemed to have that Texas hustler's talent for letting it all roll off his back. There were only rare exceptions when I saw him upset. The classic case was when they grabbed him out of his rack one Sunday morning to stand guard duty or "walk post" because someone else did not show up. It was a rainy miserable day as he walked post around the armory for four hours and then the New York Giants upset his beloved Dallas Cowboys in football that same evening. The next morning he truly was "fit to be tied", "That's the last fucking time I ever walk post in the fucking rain for the fucking Marine Corps. Ra ha tooey. And, do you believe that the New York Giants beat Dallas? You have to be shitting me! Do you know that its eight-five fucking steps around that God damned armory? I ain't never sleeping in again on a weekend. Regulations say that I don't have to draw or keep a rifle if I don't use it in my everyday duties. Today, this rifle goes back to the armory for good."

But, that incident aside, he seemed to have the necessary temperament to handle the next eighteen months of "shit flowing downhill." I clearly did not. Forty-five years later, I'm convinced I still don't have the temperament. As a matter of fact, I'm quite sure that I never want to be tolerant of that kind of nonsense again in my lifetime.

CHAPTER FIFTEEN

EIGHTEEN MONTHS AND A WAKEUP

Looking back on it now, the eighteen months has come and gone as has another forty-three years. But, back then, it seemed like an eternity staring me in the face. I wondered how I was going to get through it without going stark raving mad. It was certainly better than getting your ass shot off in Viet Nam but the day to day aggravation associated with being an enlisted man in the Marine Corps was almost too much to bear. Anyone wearing one stripe more than you were could tell you what to do at any given moment. You were at the beck and call of NCO's and officers who probably "couldn't have carried your glove" if you were operating in the real world.

But, this was what we had to look forward to for the next eighteen months. Worst of all, this was the "good news." This was the tradeoff that we had made in order to not serve any more time in the Marine Corps than we had to. One of the better stories going around in those days was the one about the enlisted man who was close to being released from active duty. The Marine Corps was working hard at trying to get him to reenlist. When you got "real short", they almost started treating you like a human being. More importantly, they started "counseling" you on the advantages of reenlisting. On this particular occasion, an NCO was trying desperately to get this individual to reenlist but he wasn't buying it. Finally, the NCO, in a bit of a pique and beginning to show his impatience said, "Okay, Smith, just give me one reason why you don't want to reenlist."

Smith looked thoughtful for a moment or two and then responded, "No warm toast."

And there was probably no better answer that he could have offered. Should he have said, "Let me count the ways.."

How do you begin to describe all the things that you couldn't stand about having someone run your life from the moment you got out of the rack in the morning until you got back in the rack again that night? It's just impossible to convey the level of anger and frustration that you feel. "No warm toast" said it all, as much as it could ever be put into words.

Even as there were some 'strange pussycats" in Casual Company back at Quantico, both Building One and Headquarters Company, H&S Battalion, MCB Camp Lejeune, had a few unique personalities to add to the mix, starting with the commanding general. The base commander was a two-star general who had a captain as an aide and a sergeant E-5 as a driver. One of his favorite pastimes was playing traffic cop on the base. He would chase down speeding cars and personally give them stern warnings. On one occasion he leaped from his staff car in front of the commissary to chew out a buck private about the way he was wearing his utility cover. The private had probably never seen a general before and stood there in stunned silence not even delivering a salute. I remember recounting that story to my wife's uncle who was a retired brigadier general. He merely smiled in amused fashion and shook his head saying, "All he needed to do was have his driver straighten the private out, assuming he felt it necessary to do anything to start with."

The general/traffic cop was eventually replaced by a General McTompkins who made it his business not to mess with the troops but rather to make full Colonels "jump thru their ass." He was one of my favorite people. As many times as I stood duty overnight in Building One, he would appear in the lobby in the morning while a detail pulled colors saying only, "Good morning, Sergeant. How's everything?"

On one occasion Colonel Jones returned to the office in a sweat after a session with the general over a personnel move he had authorized. Jones was really shook up about the session and recounted the experience to all who would listen, "The general said that I told you not to move Major Smith. You didn't listen to me. God damn it my watch is stopped. Now get the hell out of here. So I left."

He was definitely my kind of general.

Within a few months, "Blake" Webster was transferred out of our office to a Battalion Commander's slot at ITR. In a way it made sense. Webster was probably a grunt's grunt and fit in out there better than anywhere else you could think of putting him. Marshall, having already done his own personal investigation on the subject, advised that Webster had also experienced some difficulties in Viet Nam. He had apparently refused to send his men back up a hill after their assault had already been repulsed several times. That decision did not sound like a good career move. Especially, if you were in the Marine Corps, but, Marshall never went so far as to elaborate on the specific nature of Webster's final punishment, if any. In his place, ITR had sent our office Lieutenant Colonel Marv Gardner who was, at least to my inexperienced eyes the, antithesis of "Blake" Webster. Gardner was tall and lean but there the resemblance ended. He was almost totally bald and what hair he did have was totally white. He seemed to be an extremely nervous, almost hyperactive individual. He also had the habit of reading The Wall Street Journal in the office, something I had never seen any Marine Corps officer do. Gunny Tedrick added some substance to our preliminary observations on Gardner, as only he could, by applying the standard Marine Corps label of "Shaky Jake" to him and then embellishing further, "That guy makes a marine private look like a precision instrument."

There were those times when I wondered if Tedrick had a professional writer making up his lines for him. On the other hand, I had renewed respect for Colonel Gardner when he once noted in passing that he had been at the "Frozen Chosin" with the 1st Marine Division during the Korean War, "I tell you, Daley, I was never so cold in my life. I thought I would never get warm again."

The First Sergeant at Headquarters Company when we initially checked in was a decent enough guy named Pollock. He had an amiable smile and didn't seem to take himself too seriously. He noted that I was an "OC drop" and asked if I had been in any kind of serious trouble at Quantico, "I mean, you didn't hit anybody or anything like that, did you?"

Having assured him that I had not been charged with assault, he merely chuckled and sent me on my way. Pollock's tenure was short-lived and within a very short period he was replaced by a dour looking individual named Neubauer. He really was more in the true First Sergeant mold. That is to say, he was a real prick. One of his favorite pastimes was calling a formation on Friday mornings to lecture the troops on the impossibility of being able to drive your "Caymero" to Maine and back on weekend liberty, "I'm telling you that it can't be done. I don't care if you drive your Caymero at ninety miles an hour all the way. The only thing you are going to do is get yourself killed. If you get into an accident and don't get killed or you get picked up for speeding, we are going to put your ass in jail for being out of bounds."

Out of bounds for weekend liberty from Camp Lejeune was no further north than Baltimore unless you had a plane ticket in your hot little hand.

The company commander upon our arrival was First Lieutenant Petronzio, another guy who appeared to be numb from the neck up. His avowed mission was to try and make all of us "office poges" in Headquarters Company act like real marines. He would fail in his efforts, of course, but it took a while for the message to fully register on him. In the meantime, Marshall and I became a little miffed at his methods and we forwarded the warrant that was to promote him to captain, to the Commanding General, MCB Okinawa. According to the directory that we used for arriving and departing officers, Okinawa was going to be his next duty station. We just decided to jump the gun by a few months and he had to remain a first lieutenant until he got to Okinawa and found his warrant.

Marshall, who remained assiduously on top of things, also managed to determine that the assistant battalion commander for Headquarters and Service Battalion was also up on charges, having been found on the beach with a sailor by the military police. Both of them were apparently out of uniform at the time. This particular individual was a nasty-tempered guy when dealing with the troops and Dave and I gave him a wide berth for multiple reasons. On one occasion, we overheard Colonel Jones tell someone on the other end of the phone that, "I don't want him around the men."

This was a time long before the "don't ask, don't tell policy" of today's military and I found myself a little shocked at the idea that a senior officer really could be gay or as we used to say in those days "queer."

And then of course, there were the actual residents of the squad bays for Headquarters Company, of which I was a member, and Service Company, which Al Dank would soon join. Marshall, Hinkle and I had been assigned to the same squad bay, as had Doug Vredeveld, and Charles Lamb. Al Dank had been assigned as the company clerk for Service Company and, accordingly, was billeted in a different squad bay. But, there were other unconventional individuals in our squad bay, as well. Bill Gianatino was a draftee who came from a relatively affluent family in Connecticut. Bill had attended Georgetown University for a while and then either dropped out or was dropped by the University. In any event, he had gone thru Parris Island and ITR to end up also in ISO as an announcer on the base TV station. At the age of twenty-two or twenty-three, Tino's hair was already just about totally gray with only a hint of black still in it. Rick Sellers was one that you would readily categorize as a typical "red neck" from South Georgia. He had attended the University of Georgia on a football scholarship for one year before tearing up a knee and somehow ended up in the Marine Corps. He worked in the print shop on the base and was constantly bragging about his female conquests in a loud deep southern drawl. Steve Baggett aka "CID" pronounced "Sid" was a young kid from North Carolina who had grown up in the general area that had produced the great folk singer, Joan Baez. He was a terrific guitar player and kept an electric acoustical guitar in one of his wall lockers. The nickname "CID" had attached itself to him because everyone in his company at Parris Island and at ITR had been convinced all during training that he was really a plant from C.I.D. or Criminal Investigation Division. He was just too "squared away" in his appearance and manner. And now, each one of us had begun our own long journey on the vessel "Tedium" sailing across a seemingly endless sea known as "Boredom", counting the days one by one until we would once again be free men.

Marshall and I passed our days checking in officers, endorsing orders, processing warrants for promotions, and filing paperwork. Late in the day or in our off hours we would pore over an insidious red book that was kept securely locked in the office safe. Because we both had a secret clearance, we also had the combination to the safe and access to the red book that dealt with the timetable for the planned redeployment of troops upon the cessation of hostilities in Viet Nam. It detailed the projected number of divisions and air wings for the Marine Corps as well as the total manpower counts for each. I have to admit that Marshall and I were all over that book looking for some hint that we might be going home early. But the truth was there was no end in sight at that time. The generals kept telling the folks back home that we were winning the war but after the "Tet Offensive" earlier that year, there was a serious credibility gap. Before the year was out Lyndon Johnson would announce that he "would not seek nor would he accept the nomination of his party for another term as President." Alas, however, at the end of the day there was no serious "early out" in the offing for either Marshall or myself. Dave was eventually able to wangle an early out of about a month in December of 1969, ostensibly, to go back to "graduate school" at East Texas State. I used to razz Marshall about the quality of the academics at his alma mater. Being a graduate of Fordham, I'm sure I was a bit of a snob at the time. But, Marshall took no offense. He simply replied, "If you think East Texas State is bad, you should see West Texas State."

I, on the other hand, ended up serving my entire two years of active duty minus two days allotted for travel time back to New York. But, in those early days, I have to admit that we still felt that there was hope. I bet that we knew more about the size of the Marine Corps and the planned downsizing with the cessation of hostilities than even the Commandant of the Marine Corps. Probably, the most unique thing that happened in that first year at Camp Lejeune was that Marshall went home to Dallas on Christmas leave and came back married. As well as I thought I knew Marshall, that one shocked even me. I never saw it coming. But, I'll come back to that one later in the story.

For a while, Dank and I would "swoop" home to New York every weekend. The drill was pretty simple. You'd go to the "swoop circle" a designated area on the base where you picked up riders, and you would fill up your car with guys going your way for a price. It might be $5.00 per head to Baltimore, $8.00 to Philadelphia, and $10.00 to New York. The money filled your gas tank and you would meet at a pre-designated spot on the trip back on Sunday afternoon.

"Swooping", however, got very old in a hurry, especially, if you were driving to New York. If you left at 4:00 PM on a Friday afternoon, you'd get to New York City at about 2:00 AM. By the time you'd get home and sleep for eight hours it would be noon on Saturday. By 2:00 PM on Sunday afternoon, you had to be back on the road in order to get back to Lejeune by midnight. Dank continued to "swoop" with other drivers for a while but as he put it, "I got nervous when I'd go to the swoop circle and see a guy sitting in a muscle car with a helmet and goggles, a glass canopy that came down over his head, and a big clock mounted on the steering column, insisting all the while, that he could make it to New York in nine hours."

Once I had given up on the "swoops" to New York, Tino (Bill Gianatino) and I started making trips to Baltimore to date two girls that Joe Steigerwald and I had met while we were still at Quantico. Steigerwald had known Baltimore like the back of his hand and one evening he suggested a disco that he obviously liked. I don't think that we were in the place more than five minutes when Joe focused on two girls sitting alone. One was smallish and dark while the other was blonde, a bit taller, and slim of build. Steigerwald definitely had his radar turned on at this point, "Which one do you like, the blonde or the brunette?"

I'd always preferred girls with darker hair and that were definitely shorter than me. The darker girl reminded me of my former fiancé', which probably was not the healthiest of motives. At this distance and with her sitting down, I also couldn't easily measure the blonde's height, "I'll take the brunette."

It was really all that simple and that quick. Within minutes we were dancing with the girls, joined them for a drink, knew their names and phone numbers, and eventually took a leisurely drive into the country for some "heavy breathing time" in the car. The brunette's name was Barbara or "Bobby" and the blonde's name was Jocelyn or "Josh." Steigerwald's interest in Josh was obviously fleeting because I don't recall him mentioning her again after that night. I stayed in touch with Bobby and dated her a few more times while still at Quantico. It's funny but looking back on those years and all the interludes with different girls, I wonder if every one of those girls had such a carefree attitude about sex and marriage simply because they were sure that we would be gone in the morning. There would be no obligation and no commitment.

After one of his trips home to Connecticut, Tino arrived back at Lejeune driving a 1967 light green four-door Volvo sedan. The car was standard shift and had a four or five-speed transmission. At that time, gasoline was still pretty cheap and economy cars had not yet become the watch word of the day. I was surprised to see Tino driving this particular set of wheels. The only thing comparable that I had seen in those days was the famous VW "Bug." Of course we all felt obligated to pull his chain a bit about the car and Tino, unflappable as ever simply responded, "Yeah, my sister says the car is so ugly that it's cute."

Tino asked me to drive down to the Main Gate area with him in order to get a sticker for the car so that he could both drive it and park it on base. In those days, a red sticker meant you were an enlisted man. A yellow sticker was "strictly officer's territory." If you happened to be walking on the base and a car with a yellow sticker approached, you were obligated to salute it. I like to think of it as just one more "fringe benefit" associated with being an enlisted man in the Marine Corps.

When you applied for your vehicle sticker one of the MP's also checked out your vehicle. On his command, you turned on your lights and your wipers, and stepped on the brakes so he could check the brake lights. You also had to honk your horn to demonstrate that it was in working order. Tino, taciturn as always, neglected to mention that, in addition to the normal horn on the car, he had also installed an "ah oogah" horn. As we both sat in the front of the vehicle, the inspecting MP walked around the car, finally, instructing Tino to hit the horn. To better hear the quality of the horn, the MP had turned his head to one side and leaned in the direction of the vehicle. Tino with a sly smile on his face hit the button for the "ah oogah" horn. I don't know who was more surprised, me or the MP but that MP must have jumped six inches off the ground. My face must have reflected shock, followed almost immediately by a broad smile. Tino was already chuckling as the MP glared at him and approached the driver's window, "What are you some kind of wiseass?"

Tino recovered quickly and replied as contritely as he could, "Oh, sorry, I must have hit the wrong button."

The MP continued to glare and my thoughts were, "This is it. We're going to the brig."

Then the MP, probably still wrestling with the idea of writing us up, said, "Okay, hit the fucking horn and you better make sure it's the right button."

Tino complied and received his vehicle sticker without further incident.

We both laughed all the way back to the squad bay. Tino was beside himself, "Did you see that guy jump? He almost set a new world record for the high jump."

I have to admit that I still couldn't stop laughing but the thought of how close we had come to getting our ass in a sling was sobering, "Tino, you're a fucking crazy bastard."

In response, Tino just laughed harder.

And so for the next few months Tino and I made our weekend trips to Baltimore. We'd drive up, rent two motel rooms, if only for some escape from our daily lives in a sixty-man squad bay, not to mention the girls, pick up Josh and Bobbie and party for one or two days. We'd go to some great piano bars and jazz joints like "Cy Bloom's Place In The Alley", have a few drinks and dance with the girls. Josh and I both liked to dance while Bobbie and Tino were both more laid back. There were times when I wondered if I were dating the wrong girl. Bobbie was very serious and intensely withdrawn while Josh would just let it all hang out.

One weekend we were invited to the home of family friends located on a lake in a more rural area of Maryland. We would water ski at high speeds and, I have to admit, I was only adequate while Josh was outstanding. She would ski without falling until her lips would turn blue. I'd make one or two high-speed passes before trying to get cute by skiing next to the boat. Next thing I'd know I'd be going ass over tea kettle.

Neither Bobbie nor Tino were willing to risk it, perhaps just enjoying watching Josh and I look foolish.

On one occasion when we were both swimming, I tried to dunk Josh but she quickly recovered, wrapped both of her legs around my waist, squeezed hard and dared me to try anything more. It was definitely a sexy position to be in. Recognizing how suspect we both looked in the water I glanced at Tino and Bobbie, both staring pensively in our direction and said, "This is not a good idea. If Tino doesn't kill me, Bobbie will."

She laughed and quickly swam away. Again, I wondered if I were dating the right girl.

After a few months, we had wearied of the "swoops" to Baltimore. Besides, I was running low on money as well. It was then that we began to settle into that boring daily routine of work, followed by chow, a trip to the base movie, and maybe a few beers at the 1-2-3 club. For a while, I started running every evening with Vredeveld. We were really starting to crank it out. We would run a mile and a half out along the main road in about nine minutes and then step it up to run the same distance back in eight minutes. But soon, even that began to lose its luster.

And just as professional ballplayers have to hack it out through the "Dog Days of August", I felt like we were now hacking it out through the "Dog Days of Year One." As 1968 drew to a close and I realized that I only had thirteen months to go, it still seemed like an eternity in front of me.

I felt that I had run through and was rapidly running out of "escapes" that could make me forget the absolute misery of our daily lives. I had this helpless feeling of watching the world go by and not being able to do anything about it.

CHAPTER SIXTEEN

THE CHART CRISIS

One of the things that I had always admired about Marshall was his ability to kind of operate "above it all", to not let it get to him. With the exception of the time that they had grabbed him out of his rack on a weekend to walk post around the armory in the rain, followed closely by the Cowboys losing to the Giants in football, I had never seen him that upset by our plight. When we had been firing our rocket launchers at the rusty tanks in the field at ITR, I happened to point out some wildflowers growing at the edge of our bunker in the middle of all the smoke and fire that we were creating. Marshall summed it all up very succinctly in that dry unemotional style that was distinctly his, "You live where you can."

And when Hinkle and Lamb were pissing and moaning about whether they might ship us all to Parris Island if we dropped out of the OCS program his response was equally nonplussed, "You pays your money and you takes your chance."

It all seemed to roll off his back. But then came "The Chart Crisis."

It all started one morning in our office in Building One. It was now early in 1969 and I had managed to get my head around the idea that Marshall had gotten married, the mental anguish of having to eat Christmas dinner at Colonel Jones' house, and the fact that I still had a year to go before I could go home. I happened to be talking to Marshall about some relatively mundane subject when I noticed that he appeared to be listening to me but also to something else at the same time. I've always been amazed by people who have the ability to do that. My wife can listen to two conversations at once and respond coherently to either party at any given point in the exercise, without missing a beat. I must admit that that particular talent has always eluded me. My questioning look in Marshall's direction resulted in a wave of his hand as he listened more carefully to something that Colonel Jones was saying to his secretary at the time, Carole Miller, "Carole, call up Force Troops over in Building 51 and tell them to send those manpower charts over here. I sent them over a few months back and told them to hold onto them. I need them for a new study that we're doing."

The idea that Colonel Jones was doing a manpower study or that any other full colonel in the building was doing a study in their "stated area of expertise" was a bit of a fiction in and of itself. The truth was that Carroll Jones, the civilian manpower "expert", as much as a GS-11 or GS-12 could be an expert in anything, was probably doing the study and generating the numbers for the charts. But true to the workings of the Marine Corps and probably most other military operations, it would be Colonel Jones who would "pitch" the plan to the General. In fact, every other office in the building, whether it be Personnel or Intelligence or Security had a civilian "expert" in place to support the full colonel who had been designated to head up that office. Jones was a tanker and had commanded a regiment. What was his expertise in manpower planning other than taking a headcount every day to make sure that everyone was still there?

As I looked at Marshall once again, he appeared to have a pale strained look on his face, "What's going on?"

Dave shook his head and responded cryptically, "It's the chart crisis."

Puzzled, I stared at him, "What the hell do you mean the chart crisis?"

Marshall looked really concerned now, "This is definitely not good. You remember a few months back Jones told me to haul that pile of charts over to Force Troops in Building 51?"

Not sure where this was going I replied, "Yeah, I guess so. Why?"

Marshall lowered his voice now, "Well, it seemed like a long walk over there at the end of the day with those dipshit charts, so I dumped them."

My eyes widened a bit at this news, "What do you mean you dumped them?"

Marshall's face took on this kind of "aw shucks" look, "Well, I sent them to "dumpster city." I shit canned them."

That one struck home, "You trashed Jones' charts? Holy shit! What are you going to tell him now?"

Marshall seemed to have recovered his composure by now, "I'm going to tell him that I took the charts to Building 51 and left them in the lobby of the building. You know what they say. Pick a story and stick to it."

Now I hesitated a bit, "I don't know, Dave. I don't think you can make that one fly. Why don't you just tell him that you must have misunderstood him and you dumped the charts?"

Marshall looked at me as if I had taken leave of my senses, "Are you fucking crazy? Tell Jones the truth, that I threw his charts away? He'll put me in the brig forever. No frigging way Jose'. I got my story and I'm sticking to it. I took the charts to Building 51. If somebody else lost them, that's not my problem. End of story."

I just shook my head, convinced that he couldn't pull this one off. On the other hand, Marshall had surprised me before with his ingenuity. He always seemed to have a handle on what was going on and the ability to stay one jump ahead of everyone else. Somehow, he always managed to land on his feet.

Before the end of the day, Jones, as a result of his secretary's inquiries, had ascertained that Force Troops Command could not find his charts and he came looking for Marshall, "Marshall, do you remember that I asked you to take some charts over to Building 51 a few months back?"

Marshall did a champion job of screwing up his face as if trying to remember before replying, "Uh, yes, sir, I think so. If I remember correctly, it was the end of the day and I hauled some charts over there but I don't think anyone was there. I believe I left them in the lobby of the building."

Jones kind of stared at Dave for a moment or two looking for some chink in his armor or his story, "You left them in the lobby of Building 51. You're sure that's what you did?"

But there was no surrender in Marshall. As he had said, "pick a story and stick to it", "Yes sir, absolutely. I'm sure that's what happened."

Jones still wasn't sure, "Well, no one over there seems to be able to find those charts. Matter of fact, no one even remembers seeing them."

But, Dave was tough when it came to these matters. There was no quit in him, "I'll be happy to go over there and look for them, sir."

Jones was either just about convinced at this point or he had decided to "give up the ghost", "No, don't worry about it. I'll have them keep looking. I sure as hell hate to have to do those charts all over again."

Marshall started to look like his old self again, "Yes, sir, if you're sure that's how you want to go. I'll be happy to help any way I can."

But, by now, Jones had turned heel and was heading back to his office. Throughout this entire give and take, I had struggled to control myself. I thought that I would break out in hysterical laughter at any moment. But now, it appeared that the crisis was just about over. I looked at Marshall and began to laugh. Marshall was having a tough time keeping a straight face as well as I said, "You are one lucky son of a bitch, Marshall."

Marshall just shrugged, "Not a problem. It's just all in a day's work. Just pick a story and stick to it. How about keeping an eye on things for a little while? I have to go out for a few minutes."

I looked inquiringly at Marshall, "Where the hell are you going?"

Marshall just smiled as he put on his cover and headed for the door, "I have to go take a look at that Building 51. I've never even seen that son of a bitch. If Jones starts asking me exactly where I put those charts I want to have some idea as to what the place looks like."

I have to admit that that was the only time that I saw Marshall "pretty much lose it", if only for a short time. He really had his head and ass wired together when it came to covering the bases and he was not easily shaken up. But it was clear at that point that, for better or worse, "the chart crisis" was now over.

My own brush with a crisis and "Marine Corps justice" was not nearly as smooth, I must admit. Despite Marshall's ongoing success in these matters and the fact that we were dealing with the Marine Corps, I remained inclined to believe that, in the end, "the truth will free you." In the very near future I would learn that "if the truth won't free you, you better make it a point to lie."

Because we worked in Building One, Marshall and I and every other "snuffie" working in the building were required to stand duty, periodically. During the week, you stood duty as either the Staff Duty NCO or Staff Duty Clerk, depending upon your rank, from 4:00 PM until 8:00 AM the next morning. On weekends, it was twenty-four hour duty from 8:00 AM until 8:00 AM. Your job was to make sure that the building was secure and to open and close the side entrance during off hours for message traffic to the Staff Duty Officer or so that the Staff Duty Officer could sign confinement orders to the brig for some hapless soul. In as much as we were subject to the Building One duty roster we were not available for any other duty rosters. I can proudly say that I never walked post once in the Marine Corps nor did I ever stand "mess" duty.

It was also standard practice to buy your way out of Building One duty if you had other plans for the night or the weekend. The going rate was $20.00. That's where my personal "double duty or the brig" crisis began. I had been assigned Building One duty over the weekend. Because I had made plans for the weekend, I paid one of the other enlisted men to take the duty. Late on Friday afternoon I received a call from a staff sergeant at Headquarters Company advising me that I had been assigned to a Company duty roster over the weekend. My response was immediate, "I'm sorry Staff Sergeant but that doesn't sound right. I'm on the Building One duty roster for the weekend."

This actually sounded like something that asshole First Sergeant Neaubauer had cooked up. The staff sergeant wasn't giving up that easily which made me wonder if he already knew something, "So you're telling me that you have to stand Building One duty this weekend?"

It was then that I made my mistake. I hesitated and then said, "Well, I'm on the Building One duty roster but I was thinking of getting someone to cover for me."

When I said that, it was like trying to throw a lamb chop passed a hungry wolf, "So you don't have duty. Is that right?"

Now, I was backpedaling hurriedly, "Well, as I understand it, I'm not supposed to be on two duty rosters at once."

But he wasn't buying it, "I think what I'm hearing is that you were on the Building One duty roster but you got someone to cover for you and now you don't have Building One duty. If that's true, then this duty stands. You can talk to the Gunny if you want but as far as I'm concerned you're on this duty roster this weekend. You don't show and you're in a shitload of trouble."

I was fucked and I knew it but I wasn't giving up that easily. Shit! Where the hell was Marshall when I needed him, "I'll talk to the Gunny."

By the time I got to company headquarters, I knew the word was out. Most of the NCO's looked up as I walked in. The staff sergeant gave the Gunny his slant on things and then sent me in to argue my case. The Gunny stonewalled me as well. I then asked to see the First Sergeant. The deal was the same. Neaubauer had a "case" for me anyhow. A while back, he had called for a company formation for a rifle inspection, not realizing that most of the guys in the company had never drawn rifles. According to a base bulletin that Marshall was all over of course, they didn't have to if they didn't need them in their everyday work. When Marshall and I had checked in, everyone had to draw a rifle. Marshall had dumped his after they had nailed him for guard duty but I still had mine. I would spray it with WD40 once a week and wipe it down to keep it clear of rust but I never really used it. When the company formed up, only two of us showed up with rifles. I was one and the other was a lance corporal. Neaubauer, asshole that he was, didn't ask the other thirty guys why they didn't have rifles. Instead, he approached me and asked, "What are you doing out here with that rifle, Corporal?"

Of course, being a smartass to the end, I had to answer him in such a way that he knew how stupid the question was, "Well, someone said that it was a rifle inspection so I thought I should bring one along."

Neaubauer said nothing but I could hear him draw in his breath in reaction to my answer and the snickers from others in the formation. He promptly ran up one side of me and down the other about that rifle, "What's the weight of this weapon? What's the muzzle velocity? What's the caliber? What's the range? You better study up on this weapon, Corporal."

Right after that cheerful little experience, I took my rifle to the armory with a copy of the bulletin that said I didn't need to keep one if I did not use it in my everyday duties. I also made it a point to ignore any notices about formations in the future. If they caught up to me on a missed formation, I just played dumb. Actually, that's not quite true. I did appear for one more formation but that's another story.

But now I had to see Neaubauer about this "double duty" thing, knowing from the "get go" that I was totally screwed. Still, I couldn't let go of it. I was convinced that they were wrong and I was right. As expected, Neaubauer shut me down cold and now I was going to see the company commander who was a decent enough guy. But, he also felt obligated to back up his NCO's. And of course, all the NCO'S hated it when you did this to them to start with. You were going over their heads and thus calling their judgment into question. This was what was known as a "request mast" procedure. In theory, you were entitled to go up the chain of command in search of justice but there was no winning it. I was just too pissed off to be smart about it and drop it.

Neaubauer left me cooling my heels outside the company commanders office and I watched him telling the commander "the facts of the matter" while I watched through the glass panel in his office wall. By the time I got inside and made my pitch, it took the company commander ten seconds to affirm the decision of his NCO's and tell me, "Well you can take it to the battalion commander if you'd like."

And at this point I really just about lost it, "Why should I do that? He's just going to tell me the same thing you just did."

There was no question that he was stung by my answer and the implication of the answer. I had just told him in so many words that he was not rendering justice to me. But to his credit, he remained calm and patient, "Be careful now. You're about to get into real trouble here."

What he meant was he would charge me with insubordination and with Neaubauer chomping at the bit to witness it "my ass would have been grass."

I said nothing more and he dismissed me. Outside the commander's office, Neaubauer was beside himself. I'm sure that he regretted not being able to charge me, more than anything else, but, instead, he simply threatened, "You've got the duty this weekend, Daley, and I better never see anything again like I just saw in there."

Again, I said nothing, just gave him a cold hard stare and turned to leave. On the way out of the office I saw another guy from Headquarters Company on his way in. His name was Jay Jay Ripley, "Jay Jay, how are you doing? Listen, I have this weekend duty but I've got plans. Any chance you can take it for $20.00?"

Jay Jay was happy to help me out, "Sure, I can do it. I'm not going anywhere this weekend and I could use the $20.00."

I had made it a point to say all of this within hearing range of both the First Sergeant and the Company Commander, but I didn't even look in their direction as I left. It had cost me $40.00 to get out of two duties but I had learned a valuable lesson. You can't play straight if the game is crooked. It took me awhile to figure out what Marshall had known all along. The truth is I could have asked Colonel Jones or Colonel Gardner to intervene from the beginning. Jones probably would not have been willing to get involved but Gardner probably would have. But, I simply couldn't do that. The Marine Corps had stripped me of almost everything that mattered, except my pride, and there was no way that I was willing to surrender that. No way would I go crawling to either Jones or Gardner for help. Interestingly enough, I never again was placed on two duty rosters for the same period. I like to think that they won that battle but that I won the war.

From that point forward, it was a different ballgame entirely for me. The Marine Corps had me by the throat for another year or so but there was no way that I planned to do anything that I didn't absolutely have to do. If they could make me do it, fine. Otherwise, I didn't plan to do "squat." Formations were no longer a part of my world. I just didn't go. Infrequently, I might get a call about missing a formation but I would simply give them some bullshit answer like, "Gee, I'm sorry but I thought it was for E-3 and below."

To which they would reply, "Well, you better make the next one."

Of course, I never did.

CHAPTER SEVENTEEN

THE MAN WHO COULDN'T LET GO

Al Dank had always been a bit of an enigma to me. He had received a medical discharge from the Army, went to the trouble of having the problem corrected by surgery, and then proceeded to join the Marine Corps. Al was a smart Jewish boy from Queens County in New York City and joining the Marine Corps simply wasn't the smart thing to do. Not that I could categorize myself as the "poster boy" for doing the smart thing. After all, I had given up a draft deferment and a good job in the middle of the Viet Nam War, passed on both the Air Force and the Navy, and finally, joined the Marine Corps. But, Al's case was really unique. He had already been in the Army and seen what it was really like before being declared medically unfit. To undergo surgery in order to get back in and then to choose the Marine Corps, really was "beyond the pale" and made people think you had gone seriously "around the bend."

The incident in his Marine Corps training that eventually led to his "D.O.R." was almost as bizarre. Al had flown gliders as a hobby in civilian life, yet, he conceded that he was afraid of heights. During training, he had frozen half way up the sixty foot tower that you had to climb as part of the Confidence Course. Unable to go up or come down, two men had to go up and get him down. Not too long after that, he ended up in Casual Company with the rest of us. I don't think I ever did get the straight story as to whether he had been injured in training or merely declared "unsatisfactory" because of the tower incident. Whatever the "straight skinny" had been, he had dropped from the program along with Vredeveld and Lamb shortly after Marshall, Hinkle and I had left Quantico for Camp Lejeune.

When he came out of ITR, he had been assigned as the company clerk for Service Company in H&S Battalion. For a while, he and I had "swooped" back and forth to New York but that had gotten old in a hurry. The physical and monetary strain was simply too great to keep it up for too long. He then settled into the same routine that everyone else had been following. He'd hit the movies and then we'd down some beers at the 1-2-3 club, complaining all the while about the Marine Corps in general, and Camp Lejeune in particular. In that sense, he was not unique. We were all sick of our situation and counting the days until it would all be over. But, with Al, long about the third or fourth beer, he would start talking about trying to transfer out and maybe even go to Nam. To be honest, after a few beers, it really didn't sound like such a bad idea. One night Al mentioned that a quota had come through for helicopter gunnery school. You would go to gunnery school and then, "as sure as God made little green apples", you'd be "WestPac" bound.

Long about the fifth or sixth beer, we agreed to meet at Personnel the next morning to apply for gunnery school. By morning, of course, I had sobered up and I had little or no memory of our previous night's discussion. But, Al had gone to the Personnel Office to apply and he was really pissed off at me for not showing up. I tried to explain as best I could, "Al, I was drunk last night. It seemed like the thing to do at the time but now we're both sober. It really doesn't look like such a great idea in the harsh light of day."

But he wasn't having much of that, "Listen, Daley, we said we would meet at Personnel in the morning and apply to gunnery school. I was there but you weren't."

Unfortunately, I could not convince him of the error of our thinking while we were both under the influence of too many beers.

On the other hand, we did seem to agree on the fact that the Marine Corps really did "suck" and that we hated where we were and what we were doing. There was at least one occasion when we did join forces to stick it to the Marine Corps.

Colonel Gardner was working on some manpower assignments and he told me to call up and have Service Company send a certain lieutenant's service record book over to his office. I kind of pointed out that it might be better for him to call himself since the First Sergeant or Company Gunny might not be too impressed by a call from a Corporal, soon to be Sergeant, Daley, "No, you just call over and tell them it's for me."

Since, we were dealing with Service Company I took the path of least resistance and called Al, explaining what Colonel Gardner wanted. Not wanting to get his own ass in a sling, he decided to check it out with the Company Gunny who kind of stonewalled me. I tried to explain that I was following instructions from Colonel Gardner but he kind of shut me down quickly, "Listen, Daley, you don't speak for no Colonel. If someone over there wants one of our SRB's, I want something in writing or else he has to come pick it up personally."

That's when a nugget of an idea occurred to me and I told Gardner the bad news, "I'm sorry, sir, but they don't want to send that SRB over here. You may have to pick it up yourself."

In all honesty, I have to admit that I had stoked the fires a little bit and Gardner bit hook, line and sinker. He really went ballistic, "Daley, you get the company commander at Service Company on the phone and tell me when you've got him."

Of course, I called Al with my message of joy for the company commander, "Al, Colonel Gardner wants to speak to the company commander about that SRB that he requested."

At this point, Dank began to catch on, "Holy shit! You've got the colonel calling the company commander? I don't think he's here. How about if I put the XO on instead?"

By now, I was really beginning to enjoy myself as I anticipated Gardner's impending eruption, "This is Lieutenant Jones, speaking."

I replied in my most polite and neutral tone, barely able to avoid a loud giggle on the phone, "Sir, please hold for Lieutenant Colonel Gardner."

As I listened to Gardner in the next office, I thought I would roll on the floor, I was laughing so hard, "Lieutenant, when I tell one of my men to ask for an SRB, you damn well better jump to it and get it over here. What the hell do you mean telling him that I have to personally come and get it?"

At the other end of the line, Lieutenant Jones found himself getting run over by a train. He clearly didn't know why as he innocently asked, "But, sir, who are you?"

Gardner had only recently joined our office but the question added insult to injury in his agitated state as he hollered, "I happen to be the Assistant to the Assistant Chief of Staff, Manpower, and I want that SRB over here in the next fifteen minutes. Got it? Good!"

As Gardner hung up the phone I wandered in to offer my apologies for the situation, "I'm really sorry about that, sir. I know I told them who you were and all that but they just insisted that they were not going to release that SRB."

Gardner had cooled a bit and he still didn't realize that he had been set up, "Don't worry about it, Daley. These guys have their heads up their asses. That SRB should be here in a few minutes. Bring it in when it gets here."

Dank personally delivered the SRB and the two of us laughed so hard in the hallway that we had tears running down our cheeks. Al was saying, "I heard him say, but who are you sir."

And we both laughed some more. The Lieutenant had then hung up and said, "Well, I guess I don't make captain anytime soon."

At which point, Al and I were laughing so hard that we had to hold one another up. I have to admit that that one incident almost made it all worthwhile.

I happened to see Al in New York a few years after we had mustered out. He had enrolled at Capitol University's Law School in Columbus, Ohio. But the really weird part is that word filtered back to me a few years later, probably from Marshall, that Al had actually reenlisted in the Marine Corps, accepted a commission, and joined the JAG Corps. I have to admit I didn't verify that information but, as crazy as it sounds, it wouldn't have surprised me. Somehow, Al just couldn't let it go, whether it was the Army or the Marine Corps. If you were to ask me to explain it, I couldn't. Maybe he suffered from the same "hero complex" that we all had experienced at one time or another. Maybe he was deliberately trying to do something that a smart Jewish boy would not do. But, I don't think it was something you could easily relate strictly to ethnic background. After all, my mother always wanted me to go to law school. Instead, I joined the Marine Corps. At least Al made it thru law school. That probably pleased his mother no end. On the other hand, if he then decided to rejoin the Marine Corps, I'm sure that decision did not make his mother's day. I can only tell you what I saw and what I had heard and try to guess at what it was that drove Al Dank.

CHAPTER EIGHTEEN

JOHN CULLEN REAPPEARS

It was spring now. The damp rainy winter of North Carolina was over and you could feel the warmth of the April sun as you walked from building to building on the base. It was then that John Cullen suddenly reappeared. He was among the few that we had left behind at Quantico that I thought about from time to time. I was walking along a path that ran next to the Personnel Office when I saw a tall lanky figure walking towards me. There was something decidedly familiar about both the figure and the walk. Suddenly, the figure was within visual range and I could see that "long tall drink of shit" known as John R. Cullen, Jr., all six foot seven inches of him. The last time I had seen him he had been wearing utilities, a full leg cast, and using crutches to get around. Now he walked comfortably on his own two legs. He wore a Class "C" uniform with short sleeves and an open collar and the single stripe and crossed rifles of a lance corporal:

"Cullen, you are one ugly son of a bitch. Where the hell did you come from? I thought you'd either be back in Fort Smith Arkansas or half way to Nam. What are you doing here?"

Cullen smiled warmly and we shook hands, "Hey, I dropped from the program, man. I came close to getting shipped to Viet

Nam, close but no cigar. They're assigning me to Marine Corps Base, Camp Lejeune, and I'm loving that idea. Hey, I go home in less than a year."

My response was immediate. When it came to being "short", rank has its privileges", "Get in line, man. I'm out of here next January, one way or the other. What the hell happened? They didn't try to ship you to Parris Island? I heard that they had changed that policy. If you dropped from the program, you were Parris Island bound."

Cullen suddenly got a serious look on his face and glanced around as if to make sure no one else could hear what he said, "Well, it's a long story. I actually went back in the program and, believe it or not, I finished first in my company."

Now, I was really puzzled, "Are you shitting me? "You went back into the program? What the hell happened? What are you doing here? Are you telling me that you finished the program and then dropped?"

Cullen looked around again. Clearly, he was nervous about something, "I'll tell you about it later. I gotta go check in at Personnel. Where the hell is it?"

I looked at Cullen, more than a little curious about his adventures but instead said, "It's right there. You just walked past it. Are you just coming out of ITR?"

Cullen kind of laughed, "Hell no! I didn't have to go thru ITR either."

As he turned to go I said, "You didn't have to go through ITR and you dropped from the program after finishing first in your company? I want to hear about this one."

Cullen turned to go, "I'll catch you later and tell you all about it."

Cullen had been a teacher in Fort Smith, Arkansas, and, despite the "hokey" down home image that he tried to convey to everyone, you could tell he was a pretty sharp cookie. This was in contrast to a guy like Rick Sellers who really was a red neck through and through and didn't care who knew it. I could also see where Cullen had probably been a pretty good teacher back in Arkansas. Despite the Marine Corps bravado that he would put on periodically, more for show than go, there was something genuine about him that kids could probably relate to. Ironically, the Marine Corps had probably built up Cullen's confidence as well. He had come to them as a tall awkward kid, two thousand miles from home, and the first time around they almost killed him in the OCS program. The second time, though, to hear him tell it, he had finished first in his company. That had to make him feel good about himself. Still, that had not been enough to make him lose his perspective. At the end of his second pass through OCS, he was still rational enough that he wasn't going to give up three more years of his life to the Marine Corps.

Of all the crazy stories that I had heard in the Marine Corps, Cullen's was the wildest. Later, over a beer at the 1-2-3 club he filled me in and it was definitely hard to believe. A few months after we had left, Cullen's leg had finally healed sufficiently for him to be declared physically qualified. Wary of being shipped to Parris Island, if he dropped at that time, he had gone back in the program to kind of "play for time." Somehow, some way, he had managed to excel and actually finish first in his company. His platoon commander and company commander both loved him, or so he said. Then, it came time for those who had successfully completed the program to sign their commissions. That is where things got a little dicey. Not having yet figured out a course of action to avoid another three and a half years in the Corps, Cullen had folded up his commission and walked out without signing it or handing it in. When they finally realized that they did not have Cullen's signed commission in their hot little hand, the platoon commander called him in. That was when he "dropped the net" on them and told them that he didn't plan to accept the commission. According to John the "shit hit the fan big time" and they threatened to send him to Parris Island, even though he had just finished their OCS program and was about to be commissioned a second lieutenant. You gotta love the Marine Corps. You certainly couldn't argue with convoluted reasoning like that.

Fortunately, John had an "ace in the hole" that he hadn't yet played. Being from Arkansas, one of the senators from his home state was William Fulbright who was ardently opposed to the Viet Nam War at that point in time. John called his office in D.C., explained his problem to one of Fulbright's aides, and the rest is history. Apparently, Fulbright's office landed on the Marine Corps like a ton of bricks and, as Cullen described it, his SRB got a red tag inserted into it.

Being a little curious I asked, "What do you mean when you say your SRB got a red tag?"

John just smiled slyly, "That red tag means Congressional Intervention."

That one kind of shocked me, "You mean to say that anywhere that you're assigned they see this red tag?"

John just laughed and nodded affirmatively, "That's it man. I'm untouchable. Right after that they cut me orders for Camp Lejeune with no ITR in my future. I bet the Commandant of the Marine Corps shit in his pants when he got a call from Fulbright's office about this."

A month or two later, Cullen and I had to participate in what was known as the "P.R.T." or physical readiness test as part of an 'IG." Periodically the Inspector General conducts an inspection of a base that requires the troops stationed there to stand various formations and inspections or perform the physical readiness test. I had chosen the "P.R.T." because it wasn't all that tough to pass and I hated formations and inspections in general. The "P.R.T." included a twenty foot rope limb. You could climb the rope either using your feet or without them in a longer time period, in order to pass. I was in front of Cullen for the rope climb and I scooted up the rope in near record time using my feet prompting Cullen to exclaim, "Well, no shit, Daley. Do you think you could do it a little faster?"

I stood by to hold the rope for Cullen as he took his turn. I watched him wind himself around the rope like a big snake and inch up it, eventually able to touch the top essentially because of his height. I kind of studied Cullen's struggles with the rope for a minute or two before commenting, "Hey, Cullen, you want to explain to me again about how you finished first in your company at Quantico? That must have been some company if you finished first."

And so it was that John R. Cullen, Jr. returned to the "land of the living", if you wanted to call it that, in Headquarters Company, H&S Battalion, MCB Camp Lejeune in the Spring of 1969. What amazed me most was the fact that the Marine Corps hadn't even taken a shot at trying to ship John to Nam. I guess that they were so "gun shy" after Fulbright's intervention that they were trying to avoid any action on their part that might be interpreted as an act of retribution or punishment. You really had to love it when the "good guys" won one.

With Cullen back in the fold, Headquarters Company was beginning to look a lot like Quantico's Casual Company before we had all departed. Marshall, Hinkle, Vredeveld, Lamb, and now Cullen, in addition to myself, were ensconced in a slightly higher level of Hell than say Casual Company in Quantico or, worse yet, Viet Nam. To that mix were added draftees like Tino, CID, and even Sellers. I have to admit that, as bad as our situation seemed to be on a day to day basis, it was somewhat satisfying to know that the Marine Corps had failed in its best efforts to make us all "heart breakers and life takers." We had all become "office poges" and we were proud of it. True enough, we were all still in the clutches of the "Green Machine" just counting the days until we could go home but it beat the hell out of getting yourself killed in a war that didn't seem to make sense to anyone. More importantly, it was a war that didn't seem to be winnable. How would you like to be the last man killed in a war that can't be won and that no one understands, or, worse yet, cares about?

CHAPTER NINETEEN

THE LIBERTY CARD SIGNING CONTEST

When I was promoted to Corporal in the Marine Corps, the first thing I did was to go back to the squad bay and put on a jacket and tie. Then I went to the NCO club and drank half a dozen dry martinis over the next few hours. I recall stumbling my way across the parade ground on my way back to the squad bay several hours later, feeling completely drunk but also completely satisfied, now being able to have a dry martini now and again, if I so desired. In those days, for the most part, you couldn't buy liquor by the drink in the state of North Carolina. You could buy beer and that was pretty much it. On Sundays, you couldn't even do that. But Camp Lejeune was a Federal installation and, as such, had its own rules of the game. The 1-2-3 Club for lance corporals and below served only beer but the NCO club would serve just about anything you could dream up. For a guy like me, late of the Manhattan scene, that was the next best thing to heaven. Getting completely smashed on my first trip to the club was really not all that surprising. The Irish like to say, "Put a beggar on horseback and he'll ride straight to Hell." Please believe me when I say that, in those days, I most assuredly felt like a beggar.

Even though I had now reached the lofty rank of corporal there were still many indignities to deal with. For one thing, I still had to draw a liberty card from the company duty NCO every time that I wanted to leave the base. This was the case if your rank was corporal and below. For some inexplicable reason, once you made sergeant, regardless of your age or experience, you were now considered to be sufficiently mature to come and go as you pleased, absent a liberty card. The liberty card could be used as a bit of a club as well. For purposes of punishment or to make sure that everyone in the company remained in the area, the powers that be in those days would simply shut down liberty for the evening. No one could draw a liberty card and, of course, no one could leave the base. On one or two occasions when I got a bit juiced up at one of the clubs, I said screw it, jumped in my car and simply drove out the main gate without drawing a liberty card. Had I been picked up in town or stopped at the gate absent a liberty card, there was the distinct possibility that I could be facing some brig time. That was something that I had no desire to experience on a personal level. As bad as the Marine Corps was, the brig had to be worse, if that was possible, and, more importantly, it was also "bad time." That is to say it did not count against your enlistment. You had to make up any time spent in the brig.

As members of Headquarters Company, though, we did have a bit of an inside track on things such as having access to blank liberty cards and how much of our annual leave of thirty days actually got booked. The company clerk was the custodian of blank liberty cards and, for a price, always for a price, you could get a blank liberty card. You would type in the necessary information but then came the tricky part where you had to forge the XO's signature. The actual recording of leave that was taken also afforded an opportunity, again, for a price. The company clerk was responsible for maintaining the record of leave taken and he was more than willing to overlook recording your leave for a price. The going rate in those days was one dollar per day. For a fee of ten dollars, the company clerk would overlook recording your ten days of leave. I knew guys that had taken thirty days leave during the course of the year and upon their release from active duty still were credited with twenty days of accrued and unused leave for which they were paid. However, you never wanted to get paid for the full thirty days when you finally got out. That would be a bit too obvious and not at all believable. No one could go without taking any leave from the Marine Corps for a full year, unless they were stark raving mad. I admit that I was getting there but I wasn't quite there yet. And so it was that I decided that the solution to the liberty card problem was for me to have my own personal liberty card which I could carry in my wallet at all times. Accordingly, I bought a blank card from the company clerk for five dollars. The next time that I drew a real liberty card, I typed in the relevant data on my blank card. But now, came the really tricky part, signing First Lieutenant Wooley's name so accurately that even he wouldn't realize that he had not signed the card. This was how the "liberty card signing party" was born.

Marshall's new wife was named Jan Wilson. She was on the short side with dark brown hair cut in a sort of page boy style. She was certainly attractive but I wouldn't have called her pretty. Dave called her "Willy" and she referred to him as "Em." I had forgotten that Marshall's first two initials were "E.D." and that in fact his full name was Emory David Marshall. David's parents had been musicians and they used to travel and play with Kay Starr who had recorded a big hit in the 1950's called "The Wheel of Fortune." Whatever his parents' musical talents, David did not seem to have inherited many of them, although, I have to admit that I never did see him actually sing, play an instrument or dance. Marshall and "Willy" lived in furnished base housing which was not luxurious by any means but was still a far cry better than the sixty man squad bay that the rest of us called home. It was there that we met for the "liberty card signing contest" equipped with a pen with the right color ink and a case of beer. The participants included "Em", Willy", "Cullen", and myself. Perhaps, Rick Sellers was there as well but I can't really recall that for certain.

The task at hand was to accurately recreate the scrawl that Lieutenant Wooley called a signature. We began by each downing at least two beers and then practicing signing Wooley's signature on a blank sheet of paper. Each person would sign and the rest of the group would judge. The first time around there was no decisive winner, so we each drank another beer. The second time around the field had been narrowed to "Willy" and me but it was still too close to call. "Willy" and I each drank one more beer and now she began to pull away in the "forging arena." This time, there was no doubt. Clearly, "Willy" was the winner. There was no necessity for another beer before signing but, once the deed was done, both "Willy" and I each had another. With my own personal liberty card tucked safely in my wallet, I was now feeling warm and cozy. Never again would I have to cool my heels in a line waiting to draw a liberty card from the duty NCO. It was, most assuredly, a truly liberating experience and I bathed in the glow of it as well as in the glow of the beer we had drunk.

Although the "liberty card signing contest" was intended to keep me at a distance from the long arm of Marine Corps justice, I would experience at least one more close brush with a "magic carpet" trip to the brig. The primary cause of that near miss would be Rick Sellers, my favorite Georgia "red neck." It was a bit like the old joke about ham and eggs where the punch line is that "the chicken was involved but the pig was committed." I think it fair to say that in the incident in question, I was involved but Sellers was definitely committed.

For those not well acquainted with the species, it's important to note at the outset that our experience to date with women marines, with rare exception, was that they all pretty much were "sister uglies." In those days, "WM's" were actually referred to as "BAMS" or broad-ass marines. But like most things in life, it's the exception to the rule that always seems to get you in trouble. If you think about it closely, you'd have to ask yourself why any reasonably good looking woman would join the service to start with and, if so, why the Marine Corps. There were, however, a few exceptions to the rule at Camp Lejeune and that would ultimately lead to trouble. For the most part, the Navy had the best looking women. They were usually nurses or medical technicians. Because it was a Marine Corps base, all the medical personnel were Navy. For that reason most of us didn't mind the occasional trip to the medical facilities, including the dentist. Good looking women marines by contrast were few and far between but there were some around.

The comptroller for Camp Lejeune was a female lieutenant colonel. She was a little over five feet tall and about three feet wide. That is to say, she was built like a fireplug. On the other hand her staff included a leggy blonde first lieutenant who really bordered on being a knockout. I should also mention at this point that the Marine Corps frowns on what is known as "fraternization." Officers are not permitted to "fraternize" with enlisted personnel in social situations and, most particularly, in romantic situations. The Marine Corps did not want its officers rubbing elbows, much less thighs, with its enlisted personnel. I do recall that there were at least two other good looking enlisted women in the general vicinity in those days. One was a slender but very attractive black lance corporal with skin the color of dark mahogany. The other was a white country girl, with dark blonde hair and a fuller figure. I had dated the white girl once but it appeared that her I.Q. leveled off somewhere below one hundred. For that reason and the fact that she was good looking, her dance card was almost always filled. A black enlisted lance corporal named Daniels worked with us in Building One and he was really sharp cookie. He was, of course, a draftee, and to hear him tell it, he was wearing out his colonel's leather couch with the attractive black girl noted above. To be honest, I don't think he was exaggerating. One night, after "lights out", I was half asleep in the squad bay when I thought I heard a woman's voice followed by a giggle or two. As I rolled over to take a look, I saw Daniels trying to coax said young lady into the squad bay through the back door that faced the women's barracks across the road. She was maybe ten feet inside our squad bay when she apparently lost courage and retreated back out the door. Daniels quickly followed, still trying to coax her inside. What he had been planning to do with her in a sixty man squad bay with fifty-nine other guys listening in, was beyond me but you had to give him credit for his "moxie."

The incident that brought Sellers and I in close proximity to a trip to the brig had been prompted by the circumstances that

I've described above, if you will. The absence of reasonable alternatives in terms of the availability of attractive members of the fairer sex was the proximate cause as the "legal eagles" like to say. It all began with the assignment of a woman marine second lieutenant to our office on a temporary basis. She wasn't really pretty and she certainly wasn't beautiful. If I had to describe her I would have said that she was "cute." Her hair was cut in kind of a pixie cut and she was about five foot in height. She wasn't really petite but she certainly wasn't chubby either. She was well-educated and well-spoken, played the guitar and loved folk music, as did I. And, even as I was asking myself why someone like her had joined the Marine Corps, I sensed that she was asking herself the same question. Her name was Madeline and she hailed from one of the western states like Wyoming or Montana. She liked to ride and ski, two activities that I had zero skills in. And although she was certainly not a Marilyn Monroe look alike, had she been more in line with the standard for women marines, that is to say, a "sister ugly", my life might have been made a lot simpler.

At the office, we talked a lot about books and music and then, kind of out of the blue, she asked if I'd like to stop by one evening to drink some wine and play some music. My hesitation must have shown in my face but she added encouragingly, "My roommate is gone for the evening so there shouldn't be a problem."

Still I waited a minute or two before responding, "Sure, why not? I'll bring some albums like Bob Dylan, Peter Paul and Mary, Arlo Guthrie, Joan Baez and maybe Buffy Saint Marie."

Now, this was serious stuff that we were getting into here. If we were seen together and recognized, she could lose her commission and I could even get brig time under the prevailing regulations against "fraternization." At the time, I even wondered if what she really wanted was to resign the commission and get out. In any event, I went to her apartment that evening. It was off the base which made me feel a little more secure but there were so many Marine Corps types around, it wouldn't take much for someone to put it all together.

In any event, I did go to her apartment. She was dressed in jeans and a sweater, looking nothing like a second lieutenant in the Marine Corps. We drank some of the wine that I had brought with me, listened to music and eventually I coaxed her into playing the guitar for me. She played some folk music using chords more than notes and it was turning out to be a really fun evening. We even made out some but I could sense something between us that I couldn't get past. Maybe it was the Marine Corps or the difference in rank or maybe it was the idea that we were both just using each other to escape from a bad situation. In any event, not a lot happened.

A few days later, though, she invited Dave and "Willy" and me to a little party at her apartment. She even invited Carole Miller who was married to a "lifer" in the form of a Gunnery Sergeant. At first, I agreed to go but then Carole Miller asked if I would come by her house and pick her up because her husband wasn't going. I started picturing myself going to pick up Carole and asking her husband, "Can Carole come out and play?"

On top of all that I was getting myself deeper into this "fraternization" thing every minute and I really didn't like the feel of it. I decided to call Carole at home and cancel out but I never did call Madeline directly. That was certainly not one of my finest moments.

The real trouble began about a week later when I was driving back to the base from town. Unfortunately, I had Rick Sellers in the car with me and he was pretty "juiced up" on beer. I'd had a couple as well but I felt okay except that I was feeling down about the way that I had treated Madeline. As we started to drive past her apartment complex, I decided that I would stop quickly and apologize. That was definitely not a smart move. Sellers looked like he was half asleep so I parked the car and told him to stay put for a few minutes. Also, not a smart move.

Madeline answered the door, hesitated for a minute when she saw me, then smiled and waved me in. I stepped in but kind of left the door open. I started to say, "I just wanted to apologize for not making your party."

As I looked over Madeline's shoulder into the apartment, I suddenly saw the leggy blonde lieutenant from the Comptroller's Office walk into the room. She wasn't in uniform but I recognized her and I was pretty sure that she recognized me, as well. My first thought was, "Shit! This is definitely not good."

Her roommate just smiled, however, but things were about to get much worse in a hurry. Suddenly, I sensed someone close behind me and I heard Sellers booming voice, "Well, no shit,

Daley, I was wondering who you were stopping to see and she has a roommate as well."

I couldn't tell if Sellers had figured out who they were yet but he was past both Madeline and me in a shot, down the hall and closing in on the blonde lieutenant, now in civilian clothes, in a hurry. Sellers had always struck me as a bit of a "hound" and now he was definitely on her scent. The blonde backed off quickly but within seconds Sellers had her trapped between the washer and the dryer in the adjoining room. Both Madeline and I closed in fast on Sellers and I wrapped my arms around him as I both pulled and pushed him towards the door, no easy task as he outweighed me by a good sixty pounds. Fortunately, for me, he was pretty drunk, "God damn it, Sellers! Do you want to end up in the brig you stupid shit?"

Somehow I got him out the door of the apartment as Madeline quickly closed it behind me. As I passed close to her, pulling and tugging Sellers, I just shook my head and said, "I'm really sorry about all this."

And at that moment, I knew that if there had been any chance of any kind of relationship between Madeline and me, it was now long gone.

As we drove back to the base, I couldn't stop berating Sellers, "Sellers, you're a fucking lunatic and if you think that I'm going to the brig because of you, you're dreaming."

Sellers remained calm throughout, "Don't worry about it. They're not going to say anything to anyone."

That night and the next morning, I kept waiting for the M.P.'s to show up to pick up both Sellers and myself but I guess he was right. At the office, Madeline acted like nothing had ever happened. When I briefed Marshall about what had happened, he just chuckled, "Forget it. It's all just part of the game. Nothing's going to happen. No one's going to report anything. How's she going to explain your knowing where she lived? You worry too much."

That was, I'm happy to say, my last close call with brig time. Thus chastened, by my experience with 'fraternization" and with my new shiny personal liberty card tucked in my pocket, I decided that I would try to stay out of jail for the foreseeable future.

Not too many months after that, Marshall advised that Madeline had been charged with "fraternization" with some staff sergeant. The staff sergeant was at least ten or fifteen years older than her and had apparently planned to leave his wife for her. Unfortunately, his wife had gotten wind of what was going on and "dropped a dime" on them both. So, in the end, I guess she got what she wanted in any event. I'm sure that the Corps eventually mustered her out. Still, there are those moments when I wonder why the hell she ever joined the Marine Corps and whatever became of her. I guess that's not too surprising. There are those moments when I still wonder why the hell I ever joined the Marine Corps and whatever became of me. Maybe, now and again, she wonders as well.

CHAPTER TWENTY

I WOULDN'T EXTEND SIX SECONDS

Colonel States Rights Jones, Jr. was a man who truly loved the Marine Corps. He would enter the office almost every morning with a jaunty step, singing or whistling some old raunchy Marine Corps ballad. You could also hear his voice two offices away as he expounded on the virtues of the Corps, "I love the Marine Corps. I've been in the Corps for twenty-six years and I just wish that I could re-enlist for another twenty-six years."

And to that enthusiastic endorsement, Marshall would casually and quietly observe, "You betcha. Here's to the Marine Corps, ra ha tooey."

I quickly seconded that enlightened opinion in an equally low voice, "If I had to do it all over again, I'd do it all over the Marine Corps."

Of course, his high opinion of the Corps did not prevent Jones from periodically complaining loudly over the phone to his brothers in arms about not having been promoted to Brigadier General, "Shit, Charlie, I was just looking at the promotion list for Brigadier. Can't you guys push that cut-off point down a little bit? I'm going to be out of here soon and it don't look like I'm going to be wearing a star when I leave."

It was now the middle of August in 1969 and I was getting really "short." Actually, you really couldn't start counting seriously until you went under a hundred days and became a "two digit midget." I still had a ways to go for that. When you went under ten days, you were "so short" that you were almost "invisible" and you became a "one digit midget." And of course, at the end of it all was the "wakeup." You could count on waking up from what had been a very bad dream. But, still, with less than six months to go, I was beginning to see the light at the end of the tunnel and, for once, it wasn't a train. It was on such a morning that Colonel Jones walked into our office with some papers in his hand and a big smile on his face. I knew at that moment that if Jones was that happy and cheerful, I was about to become unhappy in a hurry. Our relationship really hadn't improved that much over the last year or so. It had simply gravitated into a sort of uneasy truce. We both tried to do our job and gave the other person as much room as possible. It was very simple. Jones loved the Marine Corps and he knew that I hated it. On that basis there really wasn't much more to say. Still, occasionally, he did weaken and try to convert me. On one such occasion he told me about a good friend of his, "You know, Daley, I have a real good friend who has been very successful in life. But, he has never served a day in his life for his country and I think he regrets that today. Someday, I think you'll be happy that you served these two years."

I have to admit that, even at moments like those, I still wasn't willing to cut him much slack, "Maybe so, sir, but I kind of think that I'm just going to feel like I wasted two years. Back home, everyone I know has been working, making money, getting ahead and living pretty good. Me, I've been stuck in the Marine Corps for two years."

Jones would usually just chomp down a little harder on his pipe, nod his head, and walk out of the office. When he did that, I knew that I had pissed him off but he worked hard at trying to hide it.

But now I was worried. Jones, still holding the sheaf of papers in his hand, and still smiling had stopped in front of my desk. As I stood, I could see the wheels turning in his head as he looked at me and said, "Daley, a quota just came in for "01's". How'd you like to go to Viet Nam?"

The reference to "01's" was a shorthand reference for "MOS 0141" or administrative personnel. We both knew that he was "pulling my chain" and I could see the flicker of a smile at the edges of his mouth as he waited for my answer. I did my best not to react but rather to look thoughtful and respond as calmly as possible, "Well, let me think about it, sir, and I'll let you know."

I could see a bit of disappointment on his face at not having gotten more of a rise out of me but he turned and walked out of my office, starting to whistle as he left. Of course, what I really wanted to say at that moment was, "Fuck you and the Marine Corps too."

Instead, I sat for a few minutes and thought about the logistics of the offer. I knew that standard procedure was to give you thirty days leave before they shipped you to Nam. "Staging", a form of training and preparation for the "Viet Nam experience", was usually conducted on the west coast and lasted about two weeks. Lastly, my orders would undoubtedly take me through Okinawa, before I would finally make it to Viet Nam. This was the home base of the 3rd Marine Division. In light of everything that was going on in those days, there was good chance that some outfit in Okinawa would look to pick up an experienced "0141" before I ever deployed to Viet Nam. If they were to release me from Camp Lejeune immediately and allowing time for thirty days and staging, I'd hit Okinawa with about four months remaining in my enlistment. Having thought it over for about ten minutes, I decided that it was time to call Jones' bluff. I rapped on his office door and entered. Centering myself on his desk and standing at attention I said, "Sir, I've been thinking it over and I think I'd like to accept your offer to go to Viet Nam, as long as I can get leave before I ship out."

Jones said nothing for a moment but, instantly, he knew that he'd been had. Still he tried to carry it off gracefully, "I'm sure that we could arrange for you to take leave first. Well, let's see, Daley. How much time do you have left on your enlistment?"

I answered quickly, relishing the moment, "About five and a half months, sir."

Jones kind of cleared his throat and said, "Five and a half months. Would you extend six months in order to go to Viet Nam?"

I have to admit that it was getting harder to keep a straight face and carry it off, especially after that question. Still I hung in there, "No sir."

I could tell that Jones was catching on fast but he had no choice but to follow through on something he had started just to try and jerk me around, "How about extending to six months? Would you extend to six months in order to go to Viet Nam?"

I decided that it was time to "drop the net on him" and end it, "No, sir. Actually, sir, I wouldn't extend six seconds. If you want to ship me to Viet Nam, that's fine. By the time I get there, it's going to be time for me to come back, sir."

Now I did look at him and his response was succinct and unequivocal, "Get the hell out of here, Daley."

As I recall, that was the last time that Colonel Jones brought up the subject of going to Viet Nam, at least with me. And I guess that I probably ruined his day by suggesting that no one in their right might would extend for six seconds in his beloved Marine Corps. But, what was it that he had expected me to say? There were some who had joined the Marine Corps out of a sense of trying to do the right thing. Our idealism and good intentions had been used and abused for two years. Now you're looking to threaten me with orders to Viet Nam and then surprised that I would suggest that you stick it up your ass? Where did they get these people from?

If my relationship with Colonel Jones had been cool before, it was now absolutely frigid and I took due care not to get crossways of him. We continued to give each other a wide berth. He did, of course, take his shot when he promoted me to Sergeant by dressing me down for not standing at attention properly. It certainly pissed me off at the time but I guess I had to expect it. By then, I was so "short" and so "salty" that no one could get under my skin all that easily. Actually, that's not quite true. They could get under my skin but I'd be damned if I'd let them know that. Besides, he was entitled to his shot after the orders to Viet Nam fiasco he had tried to jerk me around with. I guess that the good guys couldn't win them all. My mother used to say that, "Landlords and tenants are natural enemies."

I would have to say that officers and enlisted men in the Marine Corps, with rare exceptions and there were some exceptions, fell into the same category. They were natural enemies as well. On the positive side, however, the calendar was now working in my favor and there was nothing that Colonel Jones or anyone else could do about it, as long as I stayed out of trouble.

CHAPTER TWENTY-ONE

THE MORMON AND THE NAVY LAWYER'S WIFE

I met Ron Parrish during the last year of my enlistment. He was a twenty-six year old buck private out of Salt Lake City and, as you might expect, coming from Utah, he was a Mormon. I had never met a Mormon before but I had heard many stories about such things as polygamous relationships and how the Mormons pretty much ran Salt Lake City. Supposedly, if you weren't a Mormon in that part of the world, you couldn't get ahead in business. Parrish did advise that examples of polygamy were few and far between in the modern world however the Mormons really were close-knit and did have great influence on everything that happened in Salt Lake City.

Parrish, however, did not come across as your typical Mormon. He was low-key and fairly affable as most Mormons appear to be but he also seemed to have a streak of adventurism in him. That pursuit of the new and unknown probably had some impact on the situation that he now found himself in. Once you heard Parrish's story about how he ended up in the Marine Corps, you would have to conclude that, try as you might, there was no escaping "fate." Rather than enrolling at BYU, Parrish had decided to attend the University of Houston. After graduation, he was working in Houston when his draft board caught up with him. The draft board that caught up with him was in Houston not Salt Lake City. Following the advice friends and family he requested that his records be transferred to Salt Lake City and that he be inducted from that location. Appearances to the contrary, there was a method to his madness. He had concluded that, if he was inducted in Houston, they would send him to Fort Polk in Louisiana for basic training. Fort Polk was not considered a desirable location for many reasons, climate and swamps being foremost among them. If he was inducted in Salt Lake City, however, the odds were good that he would be sent to Fort Ord in California for basic training, a locale and climate much more to his liking. What Parrish failed to figure on was the Marine Corps.

As requested, Parrish's records were transferred to Salt Lake City and he was in fact inducted from that location. Unfortunately, he was inducted not into the Army, as planned, but rather into the Marine Corps. The unkindest cut of all was that instead of being assigned to Camp Pendleton in California for basic training, he was assigned to Parris Island in South Carolina, a location considered by some to be second in the ratings only to Devil's Island when it came to hellholes. He emerged from ITR with a "clean sleeve", as they liked to say, and at twenty-six years of age, he surely had to be one of the oldest privates in captivity. Given the fact that he had in fact been drafted and was just now only twenty-six, he must have been drafted just before his birthday. In those days, the government, in its infinite wisdom and infallible sense of justice and fair play, was drafting males without a deferment who fell into the age groups nineteen to twenty-six, selecting the youngest first and then working their way up the line. That, of course, meant the youngest, least educated, and more than likely the poorest, individuals were being drafted first. Parrish, who appeared to be an individual who would have had no luck if not for bad luck, had somehow just missed that "magic marker" for escape, age twenty-six. Upon checking in at Camp Lejeune he did catch a break and was assigned to the Legal Services Office, rather than being shipped to Viet Nam.

In addition to being a somewhat atypical Mormon, Parish also had a certain gift for emulation that was admirable. This was clearly in evidence at the very last formation that I ever attended at Camp Lejeune. Neaubauer, my favorite First Sergeant, had called for a formation for all Headquarters Company personnel residing in our squad bay. I showed up primarily because it sounded like a "command performance" and I wanted to check it out. No more than thirty-five or forty of us showed up dressed nattily in our Class "A" uniforms, as we had been instructed to do. It was only then that we learned that Neaubauer was selecting a platoon to stand rifle inspection for the next Inspector General "IG". Not yet having figured out how I was going to do it, I had already decided that there was no way that I was going to perform for the IG this time around. As far as I was concerned, my days of standing in formations and undergoing inspections, especially rifle inspections, were history.

Neaubauer seemed to have smartened up a bit since our last series of encounters. Accompanied by the company duty clerk, he started with the first man in the first squad. The duty clerk wrote down the man's name and rank. Neaubauer was determined that the group he now held "captive via formation" would not escape the IG. He and the duty clerk then moved down the squad man by man moving from his left to his right. I have to admit that I was rapidly losing hope that I might escape but then the door of opportunity opened just a crack. As they reached the end of the first squad, they moved to the second squad but instead of now moving from his right to his left and continuing to write down names, he and the duty clerk turned left and walked towards the first man in the second squad with their backs to me. I happened to be standing at the end of the second squad. As they walked the length of the squad away from me, I simply took one step forward and I now stood at the end of the first squad, trying to look as inconspicuous as possible. As they finished up with the second squad, obviously, my name was not on the list. They once again stepped forward towards the third squad, turned left and again moved to the first man with their backs to the last man in the third squad. As they did, I caught a movement out of the corner of my eye and saw Parrish take one step forward to now stand at the end of the second squad before Neaubauer turned to begin writing down the names for the third squad. I thought to myself, "This boy really learns fast."

Fortunately for the both of us, Neaubauer did not have the good sense to take a head count of those in the formation and then compare it to a count of names on his list. Had he done so he would have come up two names short and Parrish and I would have been "up shit's creek without a paddle." Neaubauer must have been certain that no one had escaped his net and he took no count. You really had to laugh. I remember all the times they made us take a count before coming in from the field in ITR to make sure that you had everyone. But, Neaubauer was so sure that he was so much smarter than all of us that he didn't bother to take a count. I loved it. But it was this talent for the rapid assimilation of information and a propensity to emulate that would eventually place Parrish in danger of serious brig time.

Working hard at not being your typical run of the mill Mormon and taking note of the fact that many married people in and around Camp Lejeune appeared to be seriously involved with people other than their spouses, Parrish decided to throw caution to the winds and give the experience a whirl. The lady that he took up with worked in his office. Suddenly, Parrish started disappearing in the evenings after chow and sometimes on the weekends as well. He never said anything but you could tell that something was going on. Although I was aware that something was happening, I never gave it a lot of thought until he showed up at my door in the early evening one Friday after work. Having risen to the lofty rank of sergeant, I was now living off base. The weather had turned cooler and Parrish, still in uniform, was dressed in his field jacket.

I looked at him quizzically as I opened the door and said, "What are you doing in this neck of the woods?"

I knew he didn't have a car so I looked around for whoever had dropped him but I didn't see anyone. Parrish just smiled, "Well, I thought I'd see how the other half lived. Actually, a friend dropped me off and I was wondering if you could give me a ride back to the base? I didn't want her to drive me all the way in."

Now I grinned, "Her? Who is she? You been holding out on us Parrish? At least, I hope she's not married."

The furtive look he gave me in response answered my question, "She's married. Shit, Parrish! For a Mormon, you sure have been getting around."

He laughed at that one and shot back, "Well, it's a long way from Salt Lake City."

Parrish came in for a while and we each drank a cold beer before I got ready to drive him back to the squad bay. He still had not volunteered anything about the lady in question and I did not press him on the subject. As we started to get ready to leave, I saw him fumbling around in the pockets of his field jacket for something, "What happened? Did you lose something?"

He kind of screwed his face up a bit as if trying to remember, "Actually, I think I left my gloves somewhere. As a matter of fact, now that I think about it, I think I left them in her car."

I stared at him for a second before saying, "That's not good. What if her husband finds them?"

Parrish didn't look like he was panicking yet, "Well, it's actually her car and I don't think he drives it. Besides, I left the gloves in the glove compartment."

I felt a little relieved for his sake but then I asked, "Why would you put your gloves in the glove compartment of her car?"

Parrish just kind of smiled slyly, almost as if remembering something and explained, "Well, there are some things that are hard to do with your gloves on."

I kind of chuckled out loud and said, "Parrish, you're too much. You can't win for losing."

Then, he looked a little more thoughtful and concerned, "Of course, there is one problem. My name is in the gloves."

At this one, I just laughed out loud, "Parrish, I'm beginning to think that you have death wish. At least, tell me that her husband is not a lifer in the Marine Corps."

Now Parrish laughed, "No, he works in D.C. Actually, he's a Navy lawyer with the JAG Corps."

At this news we both burst into laughter and I laughed so hard that the tears started to run down my cheeks. Then I drove him back to the squad bay, chuckling all the way. That was one of the last times that I saw Parrish before I was released from active duty. Whether the mystery lady's husband ever found Parrish's gloves with his name neatly stenciled in the linings or he ended up in the brig, I couldn't say. All I can say as I think back on Parrish and laugh to myself even today, he was right, "It is a long way from Salt Lake City, Utah to Camp Lejeune, North Carolina."

That was kind of the way that the Marine Corps had of changing you. Once you were in its clutches, regardless of your background and upbringing, there simply were no basic tenets of life that were not "up for grabs." Anything was possible, even if it happened to be illegal, immoral or fattening. Of course, Parrish probably had a bit of a head start in any event. He just did not seem like he ever truly was a Mormon at heart. I could just picture Parrish getting ready to jump into bed with the Navy lawyer's wife and saying to himself, "What would Brigham do? Ask if she had a sister or a friend?"

I guess that's not really all that funny, but, as Mormons go, Parrish was really something special.

CHAPTER TWENTY-TWO

MARRIAGE, A SOOTHING BALM

When I was a kid and I would fall and cut myself or scrape my knee, my mother would always have some sort of salve or ointment which she applied to ease the pain and help the injury heal. If you managed to pick up a splinter in your finger or your foot, she would apply a black ointment that she called "drawing salve" that was supposed to draw the splinter out from under the skin without having to resort to more painful methods such as sterilized needles. Whether it really worked or not is difficult to say but there was a soothing manner about the process that convinced you that you were definitely on the mend in a relatively painless manner. Perhaps, that's what I was looking for when I married for the first time, a soothing ointment or balm to help heal the mental and physical cuts and abrasions inflicted by almost two years in the Marine Corps.

We were married on November 15, 1969, when I had approximately seventy-four days remaining in the active duty portion of my enlistment in the Marine Corps. I was scheduled to be released from active duty on January 28, 1970. Although it would be easy to say that our marriage was a match made in heaven, in fact, with the exception of Pat and myself, no one else appeared thrilled with our decision. I had been born and raised a Catholic and was a native New Yorker while she was raised as a Baptist in Charlotte, North Carolina. If truth be told, in light of all the differences in our backgrounds and the objections of both her parents and mine, the marriage was probably destined to fail, almost from the start. Still, with two friends as witnesses, we were married in a civil ceremony in York, South Carolina followed by dinner for four at a local restaurant.

I had met Pat six or seven months earlier while we were at Camp Lejeune. We both worked in Building One. She had been separated from her husband for almost two years. He also happened to be a lifer in the Marine Corps. At the time, we were both in our mid-twenties. She had been married for four or five years, had two young sons, ages three and two, and was in the process of divorcing her husband. We had been seeing each other for a month or two, but, to be honest, she was a bit more serious about the relationship than I was. When I told her that, things cooled off very quickly and we soon stopped seeing one another. Within a few weeks she had packed up and moved back to Charlotte where her folks resided. I experienced some regrets at the time but, I wasn't really sure as to what my feelings towards her were. I liked her which is always a good start but I wasn't convinced that I loved her. If you are a movie fan, you'll remember that the actor James Stewart, in "Shenandoah" advised a potential son-in-law that it's important to like someone before you love them. His view was that if you liked a person you could learn to love them. If you loved them and didn't like them, you were courting disaster. You have to admit that, if James Stewart said it, you almost had to believe it.

I didn't see her again for three or four months until one afternoon she stopped in at the office to say hello. She apparently had been visiting friends in the area. I took her out to dinner and, of course, within short order we were back where we had left off a few months earlier. She invited me to visit her in Charlotte the following weekend. Marshall and Willy decided to come along in order to see the "Charlotte 600", one of the NASCAR races that had been scheduled for that weekend. Before long, I was steadily swooping to Charlotte almost every weekend. I used to ride with a Sergeant E-5 named Bogar for about $10.00 per swoop. He lived in Boone, North Carolina, which was supposed to be the ancestral home of NASCAR legend, Richard Petty.

Bogar drove a Ford Mustang. From the way that he cruised along those winding hilly roads from Lejeune to Charlotte and back at about eighty-five miles an hour, you would have thought that he was auditioning for NASCAR. According to Bogar, Boone was horse country as well. People raised horses and about once a year they had a big rodeo weekend where everyone dressed up like cowboys and rode their horses around town. As Bogar zipped his car through those North Carolina hills, it was tough to make the connection between Bogar and horses, except for the fact that his car carried the name Mustang. He would drop me at the bus station in Boone and Pat would pick me up at about eight on Friday evenings. Bogar and I would then connect up for the return trip at about six on Sunday evenings. Occasionally, I would drive part of the way back but I usually kept it down to around sixty mile an hour. Even so, there was a lot of ground fog on those roads and seeing where you were going at night was not always easy. I have to admit that I really did look forward to those weekends in Charlotte after a long, tedious week at Camp Lejeune. For a period of two days you almost felt like you were living a normal life again.

Pat's father had set her and the children up in a small house in Charlotte, close to where he lived, hoping that she would remain in the area. I'm sure that was one of the reasons why he was not thrilled to see his daughter dating a guy from New York who had no plans to remain in North Carolina any longer than he absolutely had to. Although I liked the city of Charlotte in those days, it was just starting to expand and develop. Atlanta had more or less stolen its thunder to become one of the fastest developing areas in the "New South." More than anything else, North Carolina represented a lot of bad memories for me and I really wanted to return to my job at Texaco in New York, once I was discharged. To her credit, Pat was willing to go to New York with me. Whether that was out of love for me or a desire to get away from Charlotte and her parents is hard to say. In spite of all the years in between, I'd like to think that it was for the former reason, not the latter.

After we were married, I had suggested to Pat that she stay in Charlotte until I was released from active duty but she would have none of it. She was determined to be with me. We rented housing off the base and moved everything there for what would prove to be a two month stay, at most, before our return to New York. We celebrated our first Christmas together and tried to make it a special one for the sake of the kids as well as for ourselves. As small as the apartment was, we had a nice decorated tree and plenty of gifts for the kids and we both looked forward to the New Year and what would be a short last month in the Marine Corps.

The marriage would last for all of five years and for most of those five years we were apart. Following our return to New York, we lived in a two-bedroom garden apartment in East Rockaway on Long Island. For the first year of the marriage, all of us, including the kids were very happy and comfortable with our situation. In early 1971, we returned to Charlotte to visit Pat's parents and, while there, I checked out the job market, more out of curiosity than anything else. Upon our return to New York, North Carolina National Bank contacted me and offered me a job in Charlotte for the same money that I was making in New York. They also offered to relocate us. That was a tough deal to pass up. Pat was exuberant at the news, "Vince, please tell me that you're going to take it. Imagine how much more we can afford in Charlotte on that kind of money. Everything in New York is so expensive."

And so I took the job. Unfortunately, I lasted only six months in Charlotte. It wasn't the job. That was fine. Somehow, though, I just couldn't seem to adjust to the small city life. In the end, we returned to New York. Pat wasn't thrilled with the idea but she was willing to do it. Of course, eventually, the marriage failed. Suddenly, little problems became big problems. We were arguing over nickel dime items. By the end of our second year of marriage, she took the kids to Charlotte to visit her folks and then decided not to return to New York. Her parting words were the "kiss of death", "I need some time to think."

We were separated for two years, had one failed reconciliation, and five years after we married, almost to the day, we were divorced.

As I look back on it all now, so many years later, I wonder what that marriage was all about. Was it just a case of two lonely and unhappy people looking for that soothing balm or ointment to help ease the pain and heal the abrasions that we both had sustained before meeting one another? How much did the previous twenty-one months in the Marine Corps affect my decision to marry someone with such a different background than my own? What drove her to choose marriage as a solution to her problems and why did she choose me? What was she running from? What was I running from? Certainly the Marine Corps experience was a part of it all. Frankly, I would dearly love to blame it all on the Marine Corps but, at the end of the day, I think I would have to attribute it to one of the old adages that my grandmother used to throw around, "Marry in haste, repent in leisure."

CHAPTER TWENTY-THREE

FREE AT LAST

There's a story that they tell about the kid who was in the process of getting released from active duty in the Marine Corps. He drove thru the front gate of the base on his way home, stopped his car and took his sea bag out of the car. He then emptied his sea bag in the middle of the road, poured lighter fluid on the contents, and lit it all up in front of the M.P.'s that were on duty at the gate. Unfortunately for him, he had not read his orders closely enough. When you are released from active duty, technically, you are released as of the date that you reach your home of record. In as much as there is almost always an allotment of one or more days of travel time to get to your home of record, you are still on active duty until that specified date. The M.P.'s grabbed the kid, pulled him back inside and charged him with some bullshit offense like destroying government property or starting an illegal fire or under the old catch-all in the UCMJ, "conduct unbecoming." In any event, they threw him in the brig and delayed his homecoming a bit. The moral of the story, of course, is as Yogi Berra famously said, "It ain't over till it's over."

Better yet, "Always, make sure it's over."

As "short" as you might happen to be and as much as might like to take a piss in the First Sergeant's coffee cup, the number one rule was to stay out of trouble until you were sure that you were truly out and safely at home.

Once I became a "two-digit midget", the days began to melt away. Initially, it was "ninety-nine days and a wakeup." Each day after that, as you climbed out of the rack, you realized that you were that much closer to that light at the end of the tunnel. I was hoping that Colonel Jones had noticed that now it was me whistling a happy tune each morning when I arrived at work. I was also really counting on the fact that he knew the reason for my belated cheerfulness and that it would piss him off big time. Marshall was even shorter than I was. He was working on his "early out" in order to attend graduate school at East Texas State. At this point, it looked like he would be leaving in early December while I would be there until late January. I have to admit that it annoyed me some that he was getting out that much earlier than I was but those were the breaks of the game. Try as I might, I couldn't get the academic calendar to work for me. Besides, I really was happy for both Dave and Willy.

Part of the release from active duty procedure involved taking a physical as well. Before the Marine Corps released you from active duty, they wanted to make absolutely sure that you were one hundred percent healthy. Of course, there was no compassion involved, they just wanted to be sure that you couldn't come back at a later point in time claiming some disability incurred while you were on active duty. Although I had never regained full mobility in my left ankle after the injury at Quantico, there was no way that I was telling the Marine Corps that. The first thing that they would do is put me on a one hundred day medical hold for evaluation. The Navy doctor saw the injury report in my records and asked about the ankle but I gritted my teeth and swore up and down that it was just fine. As the old saying goes, "If the truth won't free you, then lie."

In early December, we had a little going away party for David and Willy and we all got pretty drunk. With David leaving, it really was like the end of an era. At least for me, it was. I guess the Marine Corp's new policy on the handling of "OC drops" had been pretty effective. After Cullen's return to the "land of the living", we had seen no new faces coming out of Quantico by way of ITR. You either took the commission or got shipped to Parris Island. The morning after the party, Dave and Willy stopped by the office to say good bye. They planned to take a couple of days to leisurely drive all the way back to Texas. Willy kissed me on the cheek and David shook my hand. His parting words were typical Marshall, "Well, I'd like to say that it's been fun, but it hasn't."

It would be seven years before I saw Marshall again in New York. He would visit with his new wife in tow. I never saw Willy again.

As we headed into January of 1970, I was whistling more and Colonel Jones was enjoying it less. I was also working hard with Personnel to line up a few replacements. When David had left, I kind of covered for both of us but now with me having one foot in the door and the other on a banana peel, the pucker factor had definitely increased. I lined up one PFC who seemed to have his head and ass wired together and within a week or two another followed. With replacements in place, I spent less and less time at the office. When I got down to the last ten days, I would stick my head in about three times a day to see how things were going as I proceeded to go thru the "check out procedure."

John Cullen was still around as were Al Dank, Tommy Hinkle, Lamb, Vredeveld and, of course, Tino. Most of them, with the possible exception of Tino, were due to get out in the March/April timeframe. John had met a young lady from D.C. named Joanna while he was still at Quantico and she came down for a visit. She was an attractive blonde from Virginia who was also a teacher and they seemed pretty serious about each other. I wondered at the time if Cullen would ever make it back to Fort Smith, Arkansas. Just about the time that I was getting out, my younger brother Paul drew orders for Viet Nam. He had been in the Marine Corps for almost three years and stationed in southern California for the last couple of years. As a radar tech and with all the bombing going on in Viet Nam, his MOS was in high demand. He had managed to hide out pretty well for most of his enlistment, drawing relatively soft duty with the Marine Air Wing but they finally caught up with him. Because he had enlisted for four years, the odds were seriously against his "skating out" on Nam. We used to kid about who would draw orders to Viet Nam first. In those days, if one brother was in a combat zone, they usually wouldn't ship the other. Unfortunately for him, he drew the short straw. My mother was frantic about his orders and even wrote a letter to Pete Hamill who was a columnist with Newsday at the time. Hamill was adamantly opposed to the war in Viet Nam. Her efforts, however, were in vain. I remember her saying a few years later that she had spent four years on her knees praying while we both had been in the Marine Corps. In Viet Nam, Paul was assigned to Monkey Mountain, a radar installation just above Da Nang that housed the units directing the bombing of North Viet Nam by Air Force B-52's. He said that the Viet Cong were always snooping and pooping around their perimeter but they never did attack the compound.

And so the war went on. Despite a gallant effort by Eugene McCarthy and with the assassination of Robert Kennedy in June of 1968, Hubert Humphrey became the democratic candidate for President in 1968. Humphrey was probably a better man than Lyndon Johnson but he managed to get painted with the same brush. He was defeated by Richard Nixon who took office in January of 1969. Nixon's campaign pledge had been to end the Viet Nam War, and "Peace with Honor" suddenly became the new watchword of the day. Still, not much else seemed to have changed. The dead and wounded kept coming home, people were demonstrating in the streets, and, to be honest, by the time that 1970 had rolled around, I had given up hope that the war would ever end. I had simply stopped paying attention to it. Marshall and I had quit reviewing the famous red book on troop redeployment following the cessation of hostilities, months before. I was so close to going home, that I really didn't care anymore. And I suppose that apathy is the real danger of any war. If it doesn't affect you personally, you simply stop paying attention. It's also a strong argument that if you are going to go to war, the pain of it and the cost of it must be shared by all, not simply allocated to the young, the poor, and the powerless.

Now that I was a sergeant, married, and living off base, the Marine Corps was responsible for moving all our household goods to my home of record. The day before I was to be released from active duty the movers arrived to pack everything up. At the time, we still didn't know where we would be living but we made arrangements to notify them of a delivery address within a week or two of my release from active duty. Early on the morning of January 27th, I passed through the main gate of Camp Lejeune one last time, holding my final orders and my mustering out pay in my hot little hands. We drove all day through a snow storm, arriving at my folks' home in New York that evening. It was hard for me to believe that I was finally home and now all my efforts were directed towards finding a place to live, going back to work and trying to "catch up" for the last two years. I'm sure that Colonel Jones would be disappointed to hear that I didn't stand there at home and say, "I'm really glad that I spent the last two years in the Marine Corps."

My orders also directed me to report by mail with a copy of my orders to the Marine Corps Reserve Command in Kansas City. My view of those orders was very simple. There was no way that I was reporting to anyone anywhere. I had done my two years. If they could find me, they could have me. Even if they did catch up to me, I didn't figure that they could do much. Maybe they could make me go to monthly meetings but there was no way that I was going to stick my head up. Six months later they did catch up to me. I received a phone call from the First Sergeant of a Marine Corps reserve unit in Garden City, Long Island. He told me that they had an opening for an Admin Chief and, with the billet, went the rank of Staff Sergeant. Steam was coming out of my ears as I contemplated having to go to meetings one weekend a month and play Marine Corps enlisted man for the next few years but I tried to hold my temper in check as I asked, "Do I have to do this?"

He was a pleasant enough guy and answered quickly, "No, no, I just thought you might be interested."

My response was immediate and I admit now that it was not very pleasant, "In that case, forget it."

He hesitated before hanging up, "Okay, uh, no hard feelings."

That left me more or less speechless but after a brief hesitation I responded as I surmised that Dave Marshall would undoubtedly have, "You betcha!"

I then hung up the phone, not hearing from the Marine Corps again until they mailed me my honorable discharge four years later, and shortly after Selective Service had sent me my "4A" draft classification.

CHAPTER TWENTY-FOUR

WHAT HAS REALLY CHANGED?

My mother first posed the question and I have to admit that, for the moment, it didn't completely register on me. We had been staying at my parents' house for a few days until we could find a place to live. I had returned to work at Texaco almost immediately after getting home, working hard at "catching up." I was in my mother's kitchen one morning, putting on my overcoat and grabbing my briefcase so that Pat could drive me to the train station. My mother looked at me thoughtfully and said, "What has really changed?"

Of course, at first, I thought my mother was being a bit obtuse or perhaps sarcastic as I answered quickly, "What do you mean what has changed? A lot has changed."

She kind of looked at me sadly and said, "Has it? What is it that is different?"

She turned and walked into the dining room as I dashed out the door.

We were halfway to the train station before I understood. She wasn't being critical or cute. She was just trying to make me see the reality of the situation. I had just forfeited two years of my life and it could easily have been more years. More importantly, I could have ended up forfeiting all of my life, as many others had. So the question was really a legitimate one. What had really changed? What were the last two years all about? Was it about trying to do the right thing? Was it about trying to be a hero? Was it about trying to bring democracy to Viet Nam or were we all simply duped by our government and men of power? And what of those who didn't come back or returned emotionally or physically scarred and crippled for life? Who does one go to see about all the dead and wounded?

While I was still a junior in college and the war was starting to heat up significantly, I spent a good deal of time wrestling with the idea of what I should do. What was the right thing to do? One of my Economics professors, Dr. Silunas, aware of my concerns and anxious for me to enroll in graduate school, worked hard at swaying my thinking, "Mr. Daley, please believe me when I tell you that this war is not ideological in nature. It is not about freedom and democracy. It is about power and money. All wars are about power and money. I assure you it is not worth dying for."

He had told me what he thought was true but I really wasn't listening at the time.

Probably, the most difficult thing for me to accept upon my return home was that it had all been for nothing. I wasn't angry at those who had not served. I had no issues with those who had been deferred or those who had simply chosen to go to Canada to avoid service. More than anything else, I was angry at myself for not having seen it sooner. Some things had changed for me personally. Two years had been taken out of my life. I was now married with the responsibilities of both a husband and a parent. But I was still going back to the job that I had left two years before. I was getting up every morning, putting on a suit and tie, and riding a train to the city. The war in Viet Nam was still raging and the rhetoric out of Washington and in the daily newspapers was still just about the same. Despite my efforts and what I perceived as my personal sacrifices, not one single thing had changed.

U.S. involvement in the war in Viet Nam would go on for three more years. Two years after that South Viet Nam would fall to North Viet Nam's forces. And at the end of the day fifty-eight thousand Americans would be dead and in excess of three hundred and fifty thousand would be wounded. Only God knows how many others returned suffering from drug addiction or post-traumatic stress disorder. The scars on our country would last for decades. The relatively "painless" means of financing the war by deficit spending would also catch up with us as inflationary pressures drove interest rates into double digit territory in the late 1970's.

Most Americans, however, myself included, simply closed the book, tried to forget what had been a bad experience, and got on with our lives. But, what of the dead and the families they left behind? What of Jimmy Kendrick, Jim Gray, and Bill Klenert? Did their families just get on with their lives or did they look back on the previous ten years and say, "What the hell happened here? Tell me why my son or brother or father or husband is dead? What has really changed?"

Although I make light of some of my experiences in the Marine Corps, you have to go to Arlington National Cemetery to truly feel what Viet Nam really meant. In early 1989, I had decided to run a marathon. I trained for eight months beginning in March of that year and ran in the race in early November. The marathon I chose to run was the Marine Corps Marathon which was held in Washington, D.C. I chose that particular race, not because I had been in the Marine Corps, but, rather, because it was supposed to be an easy first time race. The course is a relatively flat one as compared to New York City. While we were there we spent a day or two touring the city and visiting the various museums and memorials.

I have to say that the most striking thing to me was the Viet Nam memorial. It looks like a long black tombstone and that is exactly what it is. It lists the names of all of the fifty-eight thousand dead, as well as, the date and the location of each death. If you really want to see the price of war, I recommend that you go there and walk the length of that memorial. It is not only striking it is heartrending as you watch tearful visitors touch names carved in the stone, trace names on paper, and leave small gifts at the foot of the wall, and as they do so, surely asking the question, "What has changed?"

As I write the last few lines of this book, a war continues to rage in Iraq. The United States has been at war there for three and a half years and in excess of twenty-seven hundred U.S. troops have already died. In the first three weeks of the current month an additional eighty-five have lost their lives. The various political polls indicate that two-thirds of our citizens believe that the war was a mistake and politicians in both parties are scrambling to distance themselves from what appears to be an impending disaster. The media becomes more strident every day as it challenges members of the incumbent administration on the reasons for and the conduct of the war in Iraq. It all seems terribly familiar.

EPILOGUE

Six months after I had gotten home, John Cullen married Joanna in a ceremony in Roanoke, Virginia. Although we were invited to the wedding, we were unable to make the trip. My brother Paul returned to the states from Viet Nam in February of 1971. According to his enlistment, he was scheduled to be released from active duty in April of that same year. The Marine Corps, having nothing relevant for him to do for the remaining two months, gave him an "early out". He then enrolled at Columbia where he majored in Linguistics and was working towards his doctorate before entering the Foreign Service in 1977. Within two years of my release from active duty my wife and I separated. She returned to North Carolina with the kids while I remained in New York. Three years later, after a futile attempt at reconciliation, we divorced. I had enrolled in graduate school to work on my MBA shortly before the divorce became final. In December of 1975 I married again. My second wife and I have been married for thirty-seven years. In 1972, Al Dank and Doug Vredeveld visited me while I was living in an apartment in Astoria, Queens. At the time Al was in law school in Columbus Ohio and made no mention of going back in the Marine Corps. Doug was employed in his home state of Michigan.

The Viet Nam War ended a little more than five years after I my returned home. In 1973, the U.S. withdrew the last of its forces. The North Vietnamese army overran Saigon in 1975.

Accompanying the sound of the whirring blades of helicopters landing on the roof and the grounds of the U.S. embassy was the screaming and pleading of the South Vietnamese civilians that were being left behind to whatever dire fate the North Vietnamese had in mind for them. I remember thinking of the photos of those helpless and betrayed people when I saw the show "Miss Saigon" on Broadway a few years ago.

In 1977 I received a phone call from Dave Marshall. He was in New York City for a training program with Merrill Lynch. On the first day of his seminar, he was amazed to look out the window and see George Willig climbing the World Trade Center using an invention that allowed him to utilize the tracks that window washers used to raise and lower their work platforms. Willig would climb to the top of one of the towers that day. Texaco had moved out of the Chrysler Building earlier that year and corporate headquarters was now located on what was known as "The Platinum Strip" on Route 287 in White Plains. My wife, Millie, was pregnant with my daughter Carmela at the time, but we made it a point to meet Dave and one of his fellow trainees from Texas in Manhattan the following weekend. Dave was a big fan of flat racing so I agreed to drive them to Belmont Park to see Seattle Slew run in the Belmont Stakes. There were seventy thousand people there that day and we didn't even get inside the park until the fifth race. Marshall fancied himself as some kind of handicapper and talked me out of betting on a sixty to one long shot that actually won. That did not make me a happy camper. He then advised me to bet the favorite, Seattle Slew to show. "Slew" won and I collected fourteen dollars. That also did not please me, "Marshall, are you telling me that you talked me out of betting $10.00 on a horse that paid sixty-four to one so that I could bet $10.00 on the favorite to win $14.00. Give me a break."

A week later, Dave's new wife flew in from Texas. Ellen at about twenty-five was easily ten years younger than Dave. When the opportunity arose I discretely asked Dave about Willy. He just kind of shrugged and said, "She's long gone. We just didn't feel like being married anymore."

We proceeded to tour New York City visiting all those sights that New Yorkers constantly ignore. We took the subway downtown in order to ride the ferry out to the Statue of Liberty. We toured Wall Street and rode to the top of the World Trade Center. At one point, we rented a horse-drawn carriage and rode thru Central Park. Then we walked through St. Patrick's Cathedral and, finally, visited Tiffany's. That evening, we had dinner at Joe's Pier 52 on the West Side.

Along the way, David confirmed all the stories about the Marine Corps that I had told my wife. I don't think she ever really believed me until David vouched for the accuracy of what appeared to be "tall tales." At the end of the weekend, Dave and I had both promised to stay in touch. But, as such things go, that was the last time I saw him or heard from him.

Now that I live in a suburb of Philadelphia, I still occasionally check The Philadelphia Inquirer, looking for Tommy Hinkle's byline but I've never seen a trace of his name. With his luck, he's probably writing for the Charlotte Observer or The Miami Herald. Marshall had passed on the "scoop" about Al Dank having gone back in the Marine Corps and that one really tickled us both. Dave also advised that Rick Sellers had married a woman about ten years older than he was and she really made him toe the line. That was good for a laugh as well. I guess he was just looking for a mother all along. Tino undoubtedly returned to Connecticut to live a reasonably affluent lifestyle. Cullen had apparently settled in Virginia after his marriage to Joanna. I never did hear anything more about Charles Lamb, "CID" or Joe Steigerwald, for that matter.

In spite of that lack of contact over the years they all remain indelibly etched upon my memory, as do Staff Sergeant Anthony Puida, Gunny Tedrick, and Colonel States Rights Jones, Jr.

As I watch the day to day news of the war in Iraq, the following words from a poem I had written at the outset of the war in Iraq come to mind:

> **Surely I've heard this sound before**
> **The call to arms, the call to war**
> **Pictures of weary and bloodied men**
> **Rows of coffins stacked end to end**
> **Politicians waving flags on high**
> **While brave young men fall and die**
>
> **At last it is clear how we will fare**
> **A collective voice rises in despair**
> **As we live again our recurring dream**
> **That strips our souls and does demean**
> **The price is blood and we must pay**
> **When will we learn, Soon we pray**

Excerpts from the poem "When Will We Learn"
by Vincent Philip Daley

ABOUT THE AUTHOR

Vince Daley was born in Brooklyn, New York, grew up on Long Island and lived in the New York Metropolitan area for many years. In late 2004, he retired and relocated to Wayne, Pennsylvania in order to concentrate on his writing. From an academic perspective, he holds a B.S. in Economics and an MBA in Managerial Accounting, both granted by Fordham University. Prior to his retirement, he had spent almost forty years working in the business arena. Married for thirty-seven years with three grown children, he had been the CFO for an inspirational publisher until late 1998. He has also worked as an independent consultant and spent two years in Saudi Arabia from 2001 to 2003, working under contract for an international school in the city of Riyadh.

Mr. Daley has had a strong desire to write for many years, however the circumstances were never quite right for him to pursue that goal until fairly recently. In 1999, he completed and published a book of poetry entitled "It's Still Me." In the intervening period, he has completed two additional books of poetry, a mystery novel, "Penance", and a full-length play entitled "Elizabeth's Wish."

"D.O.R." is a book about his experiences as an enlisted man in the United States Marine Corps from 1968 to 1970 during the period of the Viet Nam War. A second mystery novel "What Goes Around", and a personal memoir, "Build Me a Home" are currently in progress.